apartment living

apartment living

stylish decorating ideas for flats and lofts

Caroline Clifton-Mogg
photography by Winfried Heinze

RYLAND
PETERS
& SMALL

LONDON NEW YORK

Senior designer Toni Kay
Senior editor Henrietta Heald
Location research Jess Walton
Production Gordana Simakovic
Publishing director Alison Starling

First published in the UK in 2007
by Ryland Peters & Small
20–21 Jockey's Fields
London WC1R 4BW
www.rylandpeters.com

10 9 8 7 6 5 4 3 2 1

ISBN 978-1-84597-447-3

A CIP record for this book
is available from the British Library.

Printed in China.

CONTENTS

INTRODUCTION

What exactly is an apartment, and how do we define the idea of one in our minds? In physical terms, it is not a house, which extends from the foundations to the roof; rather, it is a self-contained living space spread over one level, or possibly two levels, in a larger building, which might be a house, a purpose-built block or even a former industrial space.

For reasons of space, supply and preference, more and more of us are living in apartments. If asked to explain the attractions, we might cite the freedom of being part of a community, yet self-contained, safely behind our own front door. Home is a place of shelter, comfort and warmth, and for many of us an apartment offers all that – and, often, very much more.

There is no such thing as a typical apartment. The word covers dwellings of all shapes and sizes, styles and colours – from the modern cutting-edge, technologically perfect space to a clutch of modified period rooms – but they all respond to the application of certain basic design and planning principles.

Whether you have always lived in an apartment or are moving to one for the first time, what designers call the arrangement of space – how to make the available space work best for you – is an essential part of apartment living. This is both a general and a particular process. In general terms, it is taking stock – working out where things should be – from the kitchen sink to the sock drawer – and why. You could argue that in every living space every element is there for a reason, but think of some of the houses that you know and love. How many of them have doors in slightly the wrong place, bathrooms that would be better situated elsewhere, possessions kept in an inconvenient place because the storage doesn't quite work? That is often the way it is in a house, but an apartment is different. An apartment can usually be planned to work as you want, the space configured or reconfigured to take account of the way you live. Each area can be planned to have its own spatial quality and personality, and there can be definition within even quite a small space.

Proper apartment planning also recognizes that, compared with a house, not only is the space in an apartment different, but so are the elements that work well there. For example, pieces of furniture that were perfect in a conventional house might well look too small, and be the wrong scale, in an apartment, where the spatial boundaries are different.

A word that is often used by apartment designers and owners when discussing the planning and arrangement of an apartment is 'flow'. Successful spaces flow rather than hiccup along; the eye moves easily from section to section, area to area; there is a smooth coherence throughout. The way in which an apartment is arranged to flow successfully is determined firstly by structural issues. For example, do walls need to come down or be put up? Are there permanent structural obstacles such as beams or pillars that you will be obliged to work around? Flooring, too, is important; the majority of apartments benefit from having the same flooring throughout, so the choice of material and colour is crucial. Likewise, any lighting scheme should be designed as an overall plan, rather than focusing on first one area and then another.

Wall colours and finishes must be carefully considered. Although it is not necessary, nor indeed advisable, to have the same colour throughout, strong contrasts between areas rarely work well; a complementary palette based on a group of colours is usually more effective. The same strictures apply to furnishing fabrics and curtains; although it would not be a good idea for them to match exactly – perish the thought – neighbouring patterns and design should be harmonious.

Such a torrent of questions before you even start only goes to show that, if you want to have the apartment of your dreams, you need to take time and trouble in planning it first. And that's where this book can help. So now read on!

PLANNING
THE SPACE

left An imaginative conversion of a double-volume space includes a gallery that overlooks the vast ground-floor area. A structural beam has not been disguised but instead used as an integral element of the overall architectural design.

right With the addition of a comfortable sofa and a children's table and chairs, a large kitchen is made into a sociable, all-encompassing living area.

One of the joys of living in an apartment is that the traditional ways of treating a space need not apply. Flexibility is king; alternative arrangements are allowed.

flexible areas

Flexibility is not simply a good idea – it is the only idea. In design terms, the major difference between an apartment and a house is that in an apartment there is less constraint to follow the pattern set by others. In an apartment, it is essential to look at the total area available and then plan precisely what you want and need within that defined space. This is your opportunity to get it exactly right for you.

It is at this point that you ask yourself – and all those sharing the space – those all-important questions about your daily domestic life. Do you want the kitchen to be part of a larger space or rendered invisible? Will you be eating there regularly or in another area or room? Will you watch television in a communal area or somewhere more private? And how much privacy would you like or need

in general? What flooring are you thinking of? And how much lighting will you need? How many baths and showers should there be? And where will you store things?

Some contemporary apartments are converted from, or based on the idea of, the industrial unit – that of the warehouse or the loft. In many of these, the area is broadly open plan and loosely subdivided into zones by partitions, screens or semi-permanent storage units that remain an integral part of the whole. In this instance, you have carte blanche, central services permitting, to arrange the space as you would wish – into whatever combination or pattern would best suit your life.

Other apartments are in converted buildings – perhaps a house, perhaps a larger space that has been broken down into smaller units. Here, there are often structural elements, such as walls, that cannot be removed, and other features, perhaps protected by law and planning regulations, that may not be altered. Yet other apartments are purpose-built – sometimes many years ago, sometimes yesterday – which can be a good thing, but which may also present challenges.

Different styles, different periods . . . but what all of them have in common is opportunities for creating flexible spaces that are fit for purpose.

below A large, ex-industrial space has been converted into a series of flexible areas that are separate yet linked.

below left A wide corridor is brought into the larger space by the addition of a dining table. A glass-panelled screen is a flexible partition for the living space beyond.

bottom In this flexible space – part office, part sitting room – the long work unit has been softened by a pretty lamp and pictures that work with the comfortable sofa.

opposite Space used wisely: in a large apartment, partition walls break up the space between the dining and living areas in a definitive but informal manner.

above A spare bed is hard to accommodate in a small space; here, a fold-up bed is fitted into a custom-made cupboard, complete with overhead lighting and a shelf.

above right If you don't want your kitchen to be part of a larger living area, installing a fitted kitchen in a secret space, behind sliding doors, is a clever design option.

top A computer is rarely a thing of beauty and it is often a problem to find a suitable, and practical, hiding place for it. A simple solution – and obvious, once you see it – is to install it in an alcove with folding doors.

When you live on one level, or even on two levels, it is easier to appreciate the possibilities of a space – how a wall could be taken down or an area broken up, for example. It is a measure of a well-designed apartment that it should incorporate flexible areas – which is not the same thing as saying that each area should have several different functions, although in some cases that might prove useful. The aim should be to create a living space that flows harmoniously from one area to another, where there is a crossover between function and design; although there may be areas for specific activities, there should also be a degree of seamless interaction.

In some apartments, particularly those in older buildings, a flow of flexible space is achieved by removing the doors, sometimes leaving the original doorway and sometimes

by extending the opening and framing it, by using a beam or even a decorative trim to define the entrance to the next area. Using partition walls, freestanding storage units or even large pieces of furniture are among other ways to separate and define the space.

However much you like the idea of open-plan living, any apartment needs private as well as public spaces; everyone needs privacy at some time during the day, even if only one room is set aside for this. Well-designed apartments distinguish clearly between the private and communal areas, keeping the sleeping and bathing spaces together in a core, separated by almost secret doors or partitions that can be easily closed off.

It is also important, no matter how cutting-edge the design and furnishings in an apartment, to have some comfortable spaces within the public areas. Observe how,

above In a large area that will be used in different ways, the arrangement of the furniture is all-important. Here, in a large loft space, the furniture has been placed in a way that allows flexible and copious seating at one end, with a flexible table area at the other.

particularly in an open-plan apartment, people often seem to gravitate, after a while, to the cosier, more comfortable corner of a room – the window seat, the bench running round a corner, the cushioned alcove or the deep sofa. Successful flexible spaces are often linked with art – carefully chosen pictures and objects can lead the eye around a room and also connect two different areas in a subtle manner.

There is a great variety of ways in which you can make the most of the flexible space in an apartment, many of which are illustrated in the individual case studies later in this book, but remember that it is the design – the elements that you introduce – rather than the space itself that is the most important factor in achieving success.

above and top In this small apartment, the designers placed the bathroom where it could be reached from any of the central rooms but could be closed off by two sets of sliding doors that fit neatly into the reveal on either side.

above left Imaginative planning can sometimes involve vertical thinking, as shown here, where a sleeping gallery has been built above the living area. Where both areas can be seen together, visual coherence is important.

right Beneath a painting by Kuutti Lavonen, oversized floor cushions sit on an oiled oak floor, in a relaxed open space created out of what were several small rooms and a long narrow kitchen, now pared down to a basic simplicity.

- If at all possible, try to see the apartment without furniture before starting to plan how it should be used and divided into separate areas. In this way, you can appreciate the whole space – especially the volume – for what it is, without your, or other people's, preconceived ideas about the total space.

- Visual links are crucial in a space that is on one level; whether they are pictures and objects that lead the eye through, or a linked palette of wall colour, patterned fabrics or floor surface. Such links not only unify but also magnify the space.

- Every apartment has a natural flow, a logical route that you want to follow through the space once you enter. Too often, though, this has, over time, been obscured or impeded by furniture or construction. Try to rediscover what the natural route might be – it will make the arrangement of both specific areas and groups of furniture within those areas far more straightforward.

- Use storage to the full and put things away! The best-designed apartment can be swiftly transformed into the worst-designed if there is no sense of order.

this page Although at first sight it appears that only the fridge is set into a wall, further inspection reveals that the entire wall is devoted to storage. This cupboard area, the depth of which was increased by extending it into the room, houses a washing machine and a dryer as well as all the food storage.

Storage may not be the most exciting aspect of putting together a new apartment, but it is certainly one of the most essential things to get right. With well-planned storage, life is smooth-running; without it, a rising tide of possessions brings chaos and discontent.

storage

The apartments featured in this book incorporate all manner of storage, both obvious and less so. There are oversized freestanding units – as much pieces of furniture or installations as anything else in the apartment; there are integral built-in systems and discreet hiding places that can hardly be seen on first inspection; and there are the make-do-and-mend solutions that we all sometimes turn to, such as baskets, boxes, bags and tins. Storage doesn't have to be expensive, but it must be considered.

Whatever storage solutions you eventually settle upon, the important thing – a point on which every apartment dweller interviewed for this book concurred – is that they should form part of a storage plan that has been formulated before the designing, fitting and furnishing of the apartment takes place, and they must be

above Do not underestimate the charms of a traditional dresser; painted shelves used for storing decorative as well as practical items always look appealing.

below right Hidden storage in a kitchen: the lower part of this island unit is made up of seamless cupboards holding all the kitchen necessities.

below centre This bedroom storage is as sleek and flush as the room in which it stands.

below left A wall of storage has been designed as a series of small units that make a pattern in themselves.

included in the original organization of the space. To wait until you move into the apartment with all your belongings in tow is simply to ask for trouble; storage can never be an afterthought, but should always be a forethought.

Only very few apartments enjoy the luxury of the extra, unused space that can be found in many houses in the guise of cellars, garages or attics, so not only should you be aware beforehand exactly what you will need to store – from the smallest to the largest item – you also need to have a clear idea about how you want to store them. Otherwise – no matter how flexible you make the space or how cleverly you have planned the layout – without the right storage, none of it will work very well, and much of it won't work at all.

left In a New York apartment, the route from the master bedroom to the en suite bathroom is a sophisticated and practical dressing corridor. The clothes are hidden behind beautifully made doors.

above left A custom-made storage unit for television and audiovisual equipment is as sleek and sophisticated as the rest of the room.

above centre This traditional and very well-designed clothes cupboard combines, in a small space, ideal storage for an entire wardrobe.

above right A simple chest of drawers has been decoratively painted to become part of an amusing, flower-themed group.

this page In the living area of this small apartment, one side of the room is separated from the other by a wall that doubles as a storage unit. On the near side, the sitting area is delineated by a low-level cupboard that also acts as a base on which to display art, objects and table lamps. At one end of the unit, a shallow set of ceiling-height shelves marks the end of the wall and holds books of awkward size.

above Good design requries no disguise. There is no need to hide this stack of the classic Series 7 chair by Arne Jacobsen, which was designed in the 1950s to be stored in just this way.

above right This angled corner under a roof has been converted into a seating area with storage concealed both behind and beneath the bench unit.

top A comprehensive audiovisual unit, which is easy to access as well as compact and sleek, has been built into the wall behind a simple panel door.

The first thing to remember about storage is that it is – or should be – omnipresent, not confined merely to the kitchen zone or the bedroom. Every area of life needs good storage and living in an apartment, where so many different activities take place on the same level, and often in an interconnected way, it is even more important than in a house that storage needs are not only carefully considered but also decisively acted upon.

So think about what you will need to store, and where you would, from preference, like to store it. At the top of the list are likely to be clothes and personal belongings, both for adults and for any children sharing the apartment; then there is food and drink to consider, as well as cooking equipment and utensils, and tableware – china, glass,

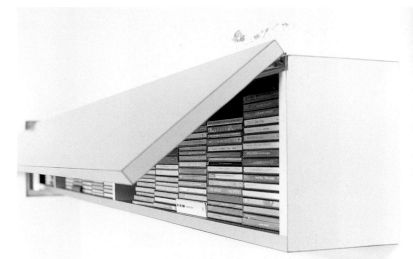

left Simple is sometimes best. This compact kitchen has close to hand every necessary utensil and pot.

right Dead space, such as that high up on a wall, can become a storage area for collections and belongings that are not needed every day.

below right A custom-made bookcase attached to the wall above skirting level does not diminish the room's overall space.

cutlery, linen and other table details. Don't forget items related to entertainment, such as CDs, tapes and DVDs, as well as the equipment for playing them; televisions and music systems are not always seen at their best in full view. You may also need to store sports equipment and accessories, from skis to tennis racquets or golf balls. And, if you work at home, you will need to find storage close to your work desk for all the appurtenances of home-office life – from papers, books and files to computers and their associated paraphernalia.

Doubtless you will be able to add your own lists to this basic one; the important thing is to identify the nature of the storage challenge because only then will you be able to meet it. Try to adopt a flexible approach. In an ideal world, you might prefer to store all your clothes close to the bedroom in a perfect fitted dressing room, but the reality is that you may have to split your wardrobe between essentials that are kept close at hand and other, less frequently worn items that are kept in a slightly less accessible place. Maintain an open mind and look for every opportunity to install an extra shelf, drawer or cupboard. No one ever complained of having too much storage!

Every apartment featured in this book includes interesting storage solutions. Some are obvious, such as using chests or

wardrobes in the best possible way; while others – more subtle and ingenious – could be characterized as filling dead spaces with combinations of shelves and drawers to create flexible storage options. There are ideas such as the secret niches carved out of and underneath stair wells, no matter how small the area, and the tall, shallow cupboards that have been installed in window and door reveals. In some cases, homes have been adapted to accommodate particularly bulky items, using previously dead space in high-ceilinged rooms. Some solutions would easily translate to a variety of living units, while others would work only in specific settings, but what all the apartment-dwellers have done is to utilize fully and imaginatively whatever space they can call their own.

above left A small bathroom accommodates a vertical unit of drawer storage, which is ideal for storing bathroom bits and pieces in ordered fashion.

left This child's top-floor bedroom has a bed and storage unit built as one; the cupboard has Perspex sliding screens that hide clutter but also make it easily accessible.

below In a corridor that also acts as a dressing room, careful thought has been given to the positioning and design of shelves and hanging space.

right A corridor leading to a bedroom and bathroom has been converted into a wall of cupboards and papered with a glamorous and arresting hand-painted wallpaper.

- In an apartment, storage should be omnipresent, not confined merely to the kitchen or the bedroom. In a living space where many activities occur on the same level, carefully planned storage is even more crucial than it would be in a house.

- Before you even begin to plan storage, try to list every category of object that you need to store – from clothes and shoes to saucepans and spoons (not forgetting bicycles and skis) – and also, if you can, make a detailed list of the actual pieces for which homes will have to be found.

- Think laterally. There may be areas in every room, as well as in the corridors, that would be perfect for storage, but which you haven't even considered. Always look upwards as well as down.

- In many spaces a false ceiling can correct imperfect proportions, especially in a converted building; it can also be an additional, very flexible storage area.

More and more in modern life, the kitchen is seen as the heart of the home, where people not only cook and eat but also chat, work and watch television; indeed, many contemporary kitchens now have televisions built into the basic design.

kitchens

The idea of the kitchen as not only a command module but also a play and social centre is just as much the case in an apartment – perhaps even more so – as it is in a traditional house. Kitchens just aren't what they used to be. Certainly, in terms of design and finishes, the kitchen seems to have moved beyond the laboratory design phase, as represented by the gleaming-white, gleaming-surfaced clinical machine. Now, no matter whether they are made largely of wood – usually dark and sophisticated rather than rural and pine – or more modern materials, kitchens are, to a fault, lighter in style, less serious and more user-friendlier than they used to be, and kitchen furniture is much more like the furniture found elsewhere in the home. The kitchen has emerged from the background and is now seamlessly integrated into the overall design of a home – which means that, in an apartment, the planning and design of the kitchen must be carefully considered, not in isolation, but as part of the whole.

If the kitchen forms part of a larger space, as it does in many contemporary apartments, the most successful way to integrate the design is to bring it forward into the room. Many apartment kitchens are now designed so that the units – both the floor units and wall-hung cupboards and shelves – are installed against a wall, but with much of the food-preparation activities taking place

above In a large kitchen area a striking dining table acts as the link between the cooking area and the rest of the room.

top A kitchen wall in a larger room is simple and easy to use, with open shelving for glasses and cooking equipment.

right In a small Paris apartment, the kitchen has been cleverly designed to fit into what might otherwise have been an awkward corner. The height of the counter hides any kitchen mess.

in a separate area facing into, not away from, the living space. This style of kitchen has evolved over the years from a run of identical kitchen cupboards into something more like a group of pieces of freestanding kitchen furniture – fridges once again hold their own, and irregularly arranged cupboards and work surfaces stand away from the wall.

Typically, such a kitchen is demarcated by an island unit. This may take the form of a traditional island or bar unit with a hob or sink on one side and seating on the other; or it may be a more sophisticated, peninsula-style unit, with many different pieces of equipment – from coffee machines to specialist grills – set into it, so that as much as possible of the preparation and cooking of food is done within the context of the larger space.

At its very simplest, an island unit might consist of a piece of furniture – for example, an old wooden dresser base, like the one

left Even in an older apartment, the kitchen can be an integral part of the larger living area. This contemporary kitchen work zone, fitted against period panelled wood, is framed by the fluted pillar and the pair of pyramid plate holders.

below An apartment kitchen does not have to be large to be efficient; it just has to be well planned to make maximum use of the available space.

in Yancey Richardson's apartment (see pages 146–55), which was literally found in the street, brought in, painted, and used for storage and a breakfast bar. Or it might be, as in Jodie Markoff's Central Park West apartment (see pages 166–71), a deep, imposing structure that on the kitchen side not only holds many essential culinary elements but also – with its zinc top and slightly eccentric, bulbous, mahogany legs – sets the tone for the whole room. Its dominance makes it clear that the kitchen is very much part of a larger picture and, to emphasize the point, a long wooden dining table has been placed directly at right angles to the work station.

above In a loft space with awkwardly shaped walls, which is dominated by the original cast iron pillars, a kitchen has been tailored to fit against one wall.

above left Simplest of storage in the smallest of spaces: pots and pans hang by butchers' hooks from a ceiling-suspended metal rack.

top left In a galley kitchen, the fridge is built into the end wall, allowing easy access from both sides.

opposite The high-tech design that characterizes this New York kitchen is softened by the bulbous turned mahogany legs beneath the zinc counter.

Although many apartment-dwellers integrate the kitchen into a larger scheme, some prefer to make the room invisible and conceal it in a cupboard, or at least an alcove, that discreetly removes the full panoply of kitchen life from the public eye. The designer Jacques Azagury devised the brilliant idea of building, at the kitchen end of an open-plan room, a partial wall open at both sides that hides the less attractive workings of the kitchen while still allowing easy access. Even more radical is a kitchen that can be totally hidden, installed either in a deep alcove or small room, close to the dining table and fitted with sliding panelled doors. When closed, the doors serve to deny the existence of a kitchen

at all; when open, they allow food to be taken to the table in seconds. This sort of solution is especially useful if the people doing the cooking need privacy and time to produce the food.

Whether your preference is to reveal or to conceal, one thing is sure: any kitchen in an apartment, no matter where or how it is designed, must always be tidy. Only those things that you really don't mind being seen by the rest of the world should be on view, so ample storage is essential both for everyday items and those that are necessary but used less frequently.

above Snug and unobtrusive, the kitchen area has been designed to blend in discreetly with the rest of the furnishings and architecture of the apartment.

left In a lavishly appointed apartment, the professional-looking kitchen is separated from the rest of the living space by a pair of imposing wooden double doors.

right Here is a perfect example of a kitchen in which everything that is not necessary is stored well out of sight. Nothing mars the perfect styling – even the wall-hung cupboards are without handles.

- Unfortunately, an apartment kitchen must *always* be kept very tidy, with dirty dishes hidden out of sight (or even, *in extremis*, washed up) and the detritus of food preparation cleared away.

- There should be a design link between between the kitchen and the rest of the apartment, even if the kitchen is in a separate room. When all rooms are on the same floor, the eye expects, even if only subconsciously, a visual connection.

- Always make sure that a kitchen in an apartment – even if it is located in a separate room – has more than adequate ventilation, including a super-efficient cooker hood and extractor fan.

Lingering cooking smells are not part of the apartment experience.

- If the kitchen is part of the main living area, use food and crockery as decorative details – a large bowl of apples, a wooden board of vegetables, a set of china jugs – that can be appreciated from other parts of the room.

Bathrooms are the new status symbols. The bathroom's role has changed, and a brand-new one is paraded for admiration in the same way as a kitchen, or more so.

bathrooms

There is nothing, but nothing, more glorious than a truly luxurious bathroom. For some people, this means a deep, freestanding bath in the centre of a underfloor-heated, sunny room with warm, fluffy white towels, and unguents and potions lining the bath shelf. For others, it means a shower system incorporating the highest of high technology – installed in a wet room perhaps, or consisting of a cabinet with electronic controls that deliver not only water flow but also a chromatherapy system, automatic herb dispenser and hi-fi speakers (one such bathroom has indeed been designed).

Whatever form of bathing you prefer, it is likely that you will be spending quite a large sum of money on the necessary elements because today the bathroom, even if it has not quite passed the kitchen in terms of cost, certainly comes close.

One reason for this is that design and technology – a sure-fire combination in terms of desirability – have reached the bathroom. An infinite variety of powerjet combinations can now offer every watery experience from murmuring summer showers to Niagara needles, while shower cabinets can deliver literally anything from a steam bath to aromatherapy programmes and shiatsu water jets. Wet rooms are becoming more luxurious by the minute, and even a relatively conventional shower is no longer confined to the size of a conventional shower tray, or indeed any size at all.

Baths and basins have changed dramatically, too. With the advent of innovative new materials and precision engineering, these water-carriers have become, in some cases, objects of

top In a small space, a striking, boldly patterned shower curtain introduces an air of élan to the scheme.

above A freestanding bath, encased in cream-coloured concrete, the same material as that used on the floor, seems to rise mysteriously out of the depths of the large bathroom.

opposite Under the eaves, a small, awkward space has been transformed into a sparkling grotto bathroom where mosaic covers every surface from ceiling to floor. One side of the room is entirely covered in mirror, which appears to double the space.

above A clever design makes good use of limited space in this wet room, where a basin has been set against the outside wall of the shower. The far wall, leading into the shower, is the inside of a curved corridor.

left In a design that combines tradition and simplicty, a classic bath with separate taps has been set in a corner between two walls of painted panelling.

sculptural beauty. There are basins in glass and wood, marble and stone, coloured enamel and moulded PVC; baths in cast iron and ceramic, but also wood and marble, stainless steel, basalt and resin; while world-class designers and architects such as Norman Foster and Philippe Starck are producing ever more must-have designs and shapes. As they have evolved as status symbols, bathrooms have become more integrated, less self-conscious, a larger part of the greater whole. All of which is good news for apartment dwellers, as lateral thinking and choice are the hallmarks of a well-designed apartment, and nowhere is that more applicable than the design, and placing, of the bathroom.

Apartment bathrooms can be small; they can also be pretty large. They can be hidden away or integrated into the bedroom. Alternatively, they can be designed as part of a dressing-room complex – an option that grows increasingly viable as ever more sophisticated ventilation and insulation systems make possible the combination, once considered toxic, of stored clothes and a steamy environment.

In many apartments, the place where you choose to locate the bathroom, and for that matter the kitchen, is dependent upon the siting of the existing core of central drainage and services; and, although this can be limiting, it can also be turned

this page An amusing combination of old and new is evident in this en suite bathroom with its old-fashioned metal chair in front of a dressing table fitted with a very modern glass bowl for a basin.

to design advantage. New space-saving designs and unusually shaped units mean that many a bathroom area can be transformed instead into two, either side by side or back to back.

Although it might seem an obvious thing to say, in an apartment a bathroom that is attached to the master bedroom is virtually an essential – even if it means having a small cloakroom elsewhere. The perfect apartment would have two bathrooms – one that doubles as a guest bathroom and cloakroom. The bathroom area could also be linked to a dressing-room area, and a narrow, awkward space – the merest sliver, in fact – can quite often be converted into a wet room or long shower room, as in Jodie Markoff's apartment (see pages 166–71), with a glass door dividing the room from the shelves and hanging space beyond.

A bathroom that is designed to be accommodated in an awkward space does not even have to have a window.

left Many different materials can be used in a bathroom; here, the double-basin unit beside the walk-in shower is fronted with chic mirrored glass that reflects the daylight from the full-length windows.

above right, small pictures Pretty, practical accessories, such as attractive soap dishes and decorative towel baskets, are always welcome in a bathroom.

above far right A small bathroom is made to look large and luxurious by entirely encasing the bath in wood.

right In a traditional interpretation of bathroom storage, a sleek run of cupboards and drawers, with a place for everything, has been installed under a double sink unit.

New LED (light-emitting diode) lighting makes it possible for the darkest of internal spaces to be illuminated on a daily basis with a wash of light as soft as a May morning.

If you are installing a bathroom in an apartment, consider making it larger than you had first intended. There is something about a big bathroom that gives the rest of the space an open quality, while one that is cramped and awkward can give the impression that the whole space is cramped. If you can find room for a comfortable chair (or even a small sofa), then the entire bathroom, whatever the fittings, will be brought immediately into the realm of the private comfort zone – something which, particularly if the rest of the flat is relatively open-plan and communal, is not a suggestion to be easily dismissed.

below left The ultimate New York bathroom experience: metal, mirrors, luxury and an amazing view of the Empire State Building. Who could ask for more?

below The style of this double basin, with its granite top, two inset bowls and long metal towel rail running underneath, is simple but smart.

bottom A bathroom can absorb any style; this one is glamorous and moody with its low-level lighting, black-encased bath and black-painted louvred shutters.

right A long narrow room has been artfully transformed into an efficient bathroom, with basins against one wall, a shower at the end and neat slatted glass shelves tucked into the reveal between the two.

- If the bathrooms are internal, make sure at an early planning stage that any electrically operated ventilation is silent enough not to disturb the inhabitants – particularly during the night.

- As with kitchens, bathrooms in an apartment should have some visual design link with the rest of the space. A period bathroom with reproduction old brass taps and stained wooden bath panels would look very odd in an otherwise ultra-modern design.

- Again as with a kitchen, an apartment bathroom must be kept tidy and clean; unwashed baths and tide marks around the bath or basin are extremely uninviting.

- Storage for necessities such as towels and soap is essential in an apartment bathroom. Ensure that adequate shelving, drawers and cupboards are included in the initial design.

THE
APARTMENTS

1
SMALL SPACES
& CLEVER
CONVERSIONS

TRICKS OF SCALE

An apartment is defined not by its size but rather by how successfully it fits its purpose, which in this case is a good thing since this apartment in Copenhagen, belonging to stylist Sidsel Zachariassen, can only be described as tiny.

below Sturdy black wooden shelves run the length of the wall, creating a storage space for books and essentials and a surface for displaying art and objects. Setting them above the floor makes the room seem larger than it is.

Sidsel's apartment consists of a living and dining room with an open kitchen area on one side; a bedroom that can also become part of the larger living area; and a tiny bathroom that is a wet room and a lavatory in one. Although the ground area is small, the overall feeling is not one of claustrophobia. Sidsel has organized the space so imaginatively, and the design itself is so simple, that everything works like a charm.

The front door opens directly into the main room, where the discipline of design and coordination of colour are striking – there is not much colour actually, for black and white are dominant, with just the odd touches of rather subtle, unusual colour that serve to highlight the monochrome scheme. The floor throughout the apartment is painted gloss white – definitely a favourite finish in Denmark – apart from the floor within the kitchen area, which has been covered in a bold design of black and white patterned linoleum. It might be thought that such a pattern would be too strong, that such a definite design would dominate the rest of the room, but, in fact, the opposite is true.

opposite The dining and working area is set apart from the very restricted kitchen zone by a wide, D-ended unit that acts as a breakfast bar as well as providing storage.

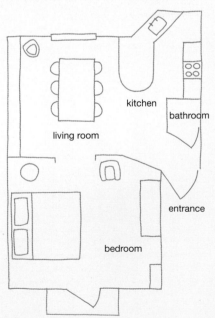

this picture Sidsel Zachariassen has managed to include a large number of items in this room without its feeling overcrowded or cramped. Like many people, she admires 20th-century Scandinavian design; both the chairs and the overhead light are good examples. A monochrome colour palette was essential to the sense of space and light.

The design marks out the kitchen area, and makes the remainder of the room look larger by comparison. The kitchen equipment is ranged against the far wall, and a high-gloss, curved, black-topped island unit divides and separates the area. In a clever touch, the side of the unit that faces the rest of the room has been painted the same white as the other walls. A large part of the floor space in the other part of the room is occupied by a long white table, used for working and eating meals, flanked by Arne Jacobsen chairs in moulded plywood.

On the far wall are two long, wooden display and storage shelves stacked with

above The juxtaposition of objects of contrasting scales – the wonderful oversized teacup on a table that barely holds it – is one of the techniques Sidsel uses to trick the eye into thinking the space is larger than it is.

left Each piece has been carefully chosen to fit into the overall monochrome scheme – even the leather bucket used for storing papers harmonizes with all the other objects. The white Venus chair is by Börje Johanson.

right Subtle colour combinations distinguish the bedroom, where one wall and the sliding door are papered in a pale leafy design. The fabric used to make the bedcover and curtains features a raised black and white and pale green stripe.

- ❏ **Use simple colour contrasts or no colour at all in a very small space such as this.**

- ❏ **Be bold. There is no room for indecisive design or decorative decisions in an area where every centimetre counts.**

- ❏ **Edit down. Be reminded of the joys of living without excessive belongings. Nothing in this apartment, whether for work or pleasure, is unnecessary.**

left Storage as display? Or display as storage? Whichever it is, the Op Art bag hanging from a pair of antlers is as decorative as it is practical.

books, magazines and other items. These shelves run the length of the room and are finished in black – naturally. They are attached to the wall at waist height, rather than at floor level; this simple device, a variation of the floating skirting so loved by minimalist architects, maximizes the perceived floor space as well as enlarging the actual space, since the eye sees a clear run of floor from wall to wall.

At the other end of the room, a sliding panel door, painted white on the living-room side and papered in a bold leaf design on the other, leads through to the bedroom, which is dominated by the bed, with a clothes cupboard standing against the opposite wall. The bed is covered in a raised-velvet black and white striped material, and piled high with cushions, so that it can be also used as a oversized seat or sofa, rather in the style of a luxurious Turkish divan. The neighbouring window has curtains made from the same raised-velvet stripe as the bedspread, and lined with a pale green cotton, which gives a cool aqueous glow to the room.

Throughout the flat the design touches are kept to a telling minimum. As a lover of Scandinavian furniture design, Sidsel has collected several distinctive pieces, including the moulded Venus chair by Johanson. Decorative details are few but full of impact: an oversized Mad Hatter's teacup is on a table in the bedroom; a black and white chequered handbag, hung on the wall, is used for both storage and display; and, in a nod towards pop art, an intricate black and white vase is carefully placed on the black and white floor of the kitchen. All of which goes to show that, although an apartment might be short on square metres, it can be long on good ideas.

this picture The optical effect of a grey and white striped wall, combined with the sophisticated luxury of the raised striped velvet fabric used in the curtains and on the bed, give a depth to what is actually a very small room.

LIGHT & HEIGHT

This is a small, very small, apartment on a garden square in London's Bayswater, but it is arranged in such a way that your first impression on entering the main room is that there is plenty of room for everyone and everything.

The apartment's owner is Ebba Thott, an interior designer whose London company Sigmar specializes in Scandinavian design. Ebba knew from the beginning exactly what she wanted. 'Like most people, I always need more space, because it's so difficult to squeeze a lot into something small. I looked at about thirty places and soon realized that I wouldn't be able to get something as large as I'd have liked; so I decided to look for somewhere that was as light as possible and also had enough height for me to go upwards as well as sideways and across.'

In the living room – and it is a room that embraces all aspects of living – there is against one wall a tiny kitchen with a hob, sink and wall-mounted cupboards, above which are two oversized rattan boxes that provide extra storage. Beside the kitchen unit is the fridge, set into a niche made by bringing the door frame forward. The new space

above far left The working corner of the all-purpose shelf that runs across the room is used by Ebba for a rotating display of photographs of her family and friends. Lights are set beneath the shelf to downlight the floor.

above left At the other side of the room a narrow table, with an overhead light designed in the 1940s, is a linear contrast to the sofa and chairs arranged around the fire.

opposite The seating area is both comfortable and flexible, with the focal point being a fireplace set at shelf level rather than at floor level as might be expected.

right This built-out corner has the television on the near side and the bathroom on the other. Small horizontal windows give some daylight to the internal bathroom.

far right An overview of the far side of the room shows the wallpapered screen in the corner. The old display cabinets with Ebba's collection of shoes make a kind of artwork, as do her grouped hats above.

above the door offers scope for even more storage, with a nifty slide-out metal ladder for easy access. Even more storage cupboards run along the top of the internal bathroom that extends into the room, and which has two high-set horizontal windows that bring the light in from the living room. 'It also means that when you are in the bathroom, you don't feel completely cut off,' says Ebba.

Ebba likes a room to have focal points. The electrics have all been hidden, and the television has been installed on the bathroom wall, below the horizontal windows. In another area, Ebba moved the fireplace halfway up a wall so she could run a long, deep shelf beneath it that stretches from one end of the room to the other; lighting is installed under the shelf. At the far end – in a good example of simple multifunctional design – the shelf

becomes a desk. Two small shelves above the desk area are used to display family photographs and mementos, which Ebba changes regularly. 'I bring out photos of people on their birthdays or when I have just been talking to them – it creates movement, which is important.'

According to Ebba, the secret of living happily in a small apartment is to create storage space for as many possessions as possible but also to use display as an alternative storage method. This works with shoes, for example: 'I have a major shoe collection and I decided to store them where they could be seen – in a glass-fronted cupboard that looks like an old-fashioned shop fixture. I thought they would look good as visual objects.' Ebba's hats, hung on oversized pegs on the wall above the shoe shelves, are subject to the same treatment. Her books also are

above A permanent sliding ladder gives access to another hidden storage space above the bathroom; no centimetre of space is wasted.

left The kitchen end of the living room makes use of every inch of space including the high ceilings. Above the wall cabinets are baskets holding occasional necessities; above the oven are recipe books and wine.

right The small bedroom is simply a sleeping and storage area with carefully chosen, dyed lace curtains that exclude the rather uninspiring view.

❑ **More thought has been given to storage in this apartment than to almost any other aspect of design.**

❑ **Storage as display has been taken to new heights; shoes and hats have been stored to create an amusing focal point of the room, rather than just as a practical expedient.**

❑ **The siting of the bathroom with its clever narrow horizontal windows shows that internal bathrooms do not have to be dreary holes.**

stored in unconventional fashion. 'I didn't want to have book shelves, and I don't like keeping books on the floor,' she says, so she piled them, very specifically, onto a low storage shelf between the two sofas.

Near the window a screen, covered with wallpaper, creates a secret hiding place for anything Ebba may not have managed to store elsewhere, such as folding chairs for the balcony. The screen also introduces pattern to a room where the decorative treatment has generally been kept very simple. The deliberately severe design of the curtains and the pelmet, which raises the curtains almost to the height of the ceiling, emphasizes the architectural strength of the arched Victorian windows, which do a great job of framing the leafy square outside.

The furniture in Ebba's apartment is carefully considered and chosen. Many pieces are interesting examples of 20th-century Scandinavian design, Ebba's inspiration in her interior design work. 'If you live mainly in one room, you need to create pools of warmth and rooms within rooms, using light and colour,' she says. 'The colours that I've used here are very personal – my colours.' The palette embraces pale yellows, stone and a brownish avocado that contrasts with the stronger tones; floors of rosewood add extra warmth. It was possible to have a dark wooden floor because the ceilings are so high. 'Low ceilings don't benefit from dark floors,' says Ebba.

In the small bedroom, space really is at a premium. Running along the back of the bed is a lip, and on either side are integral rounded side tables; beneath the mattress are pull-out blanket and linen drawers. The wall by the bed is dedicated to hanging and shelving space.

The bedroom window looks out onto an unlovely view of Bayswater, so, to disguise the landscape, Ebba has hung a panel of antique French lace, which she has dyed black, and which diffuses, softly, the outline of the buildings beyond.

Throughout this flat, so homely and comfortable, there is a conscious thought process that has informed every aspect of Ebba's apartment life.

GLAMOROUS POD

Not long ago, this sleek, contemporary, top-floor apartment in Paris was no more than two ramshackle studios that had been converted into an oddly planned home of little appeal.

right On the far side of the central pod is the bedroom with its exposed beams. The room has been left doorless so that it can be incorporated when necessary into the larger scheme.

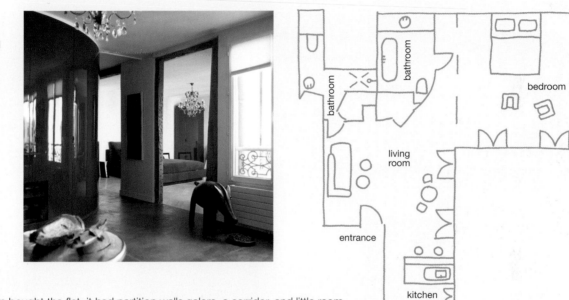

When Andre Cohen bought the flat, it had partition walls galore, a corridor, and little room for manoeuvre. He brought in Parisian architect Marianne Pascal to change this muddled space into something that he and his partner could use on their frequent trips to Paris – 'a large hotel room', he says now, but of course he wanted, and got, far more than that.

Once, the front door led into a space divided up into small segments with a corridor seemingly linking them. What Andre wanted instead was a living area, a kitchen that 'wasn't too much like a kitchen' and a bedroom that somehow worked with the rest of the apartment. In the original flat, the bedroom was separate, but it was obvious that better use could be made of the limited space if the bedroom could be made to connect with the rest of the flat. As Andre says, 'It was important that the bedroom became an area that could be used, if necessary, as an extension of the living area, and that the bed was not too bed-like so that, when we had parties, guests would feel happy about sitting there.' So the decision was made to open the bedroom up and make a

opposite As you enter the front door of this tiny Paris apartment, you are greeted by this view of an all-encompassing red pod that houses storage and bathrooms and is the key to the entire space.

space that was linked with the rest of the apartment. It was deliberately furnished in a way that, although comfortable, was not overtly bedroom-like; the bed slides back and reveals a hollow base with a drawer inside to hold bedclothes and extra linen.

The semi-open bedroom also raised the issue of peace and quiet. The original design plan was to have the kitchen on the left of the entrance and put a small salon where the kitchen now is. The new arrangement means that, if Andre wants to get up early, he can make his breakfast and use his computer without disturbing any late sleeper in the bedroom.

The design brief also stipulated that maximum use should be made of the space, that the lines should be clean and, most importantly, that all the functional and practical aspects of the apartment should be hidden from view so as not to obstruct this new, clean-lined space. Although the area is relatively small, this concealment of paraphernalia wasn't a simple problem to solve. For a start nothing was flat or even, so straightforward storage units would not necessarily work. Various options were discussed until Marianne came up with the idea of installing one big, central piece that would hold everything, including the bathrooms. This line of thought led to the birth of the pod – basically a curved wall with cupboards inside. It sounds simple and, indeed, the idea is simple – but the finished piece is much more impressive than such a description implies.

The curve encircles and encloses a large part of the centre of the apartment. Viewed from the living area, the lacquered pod takes the eye round the apartment, encompassing the bedroom, and curves round the shower and lavatory on one side and the bathroom on the other.

A curved shape was chosen because, as Marianne says, 'It was easier to put everything in a curve rather than having several straight angles – the eye cannot follow angles in the same way.' It was also easier for the circulation of human traffic, and would give an unity to the apartment, linking the different zones together.

So the curved red laminate wall with its internal divisions and invisible doors was made and installed, and suddenly

left The view of the living area from the bedroom shows an elongated seating area, directly inside the front door, that maximizes the floor space. The matt-concrete floor acts as a textural contrast to the glossy surface of the pod.

this page Like everything in this small apartment, the bedroom is full of surprises. The original oak strip floor was uncovered and restored. A gas fire, brought from England, was installed in the old fireplace. Beside it stands a tall storage unit in the same glossy red as the central pod.

above The bed was deliberately chosen not to be 'bed-like' so that, when Andre is entertaining guests, the bedroom can be used as an additional seating area – a second sitting room.

right Between the two spaces framed by the original beams that were once doors is an open storage unit for books that has a sculptural quality.

❑ **Although there is a great deal of colour in this apartment, it is used with care and thought.**

❑ **Decorative objects of all shapes and sizes are used in every room; but, again, each object has been chosen carefully to work together and within the overall design.**

❑ **Contrary to received wisdom, there are different floor surfaces in this apartment, of concrete and wood. One reason they work together is that the bedroom floor is slightly higher than that in the living room.**

everything else fell into place – the fireplace, for example. 'We wanted a fireplace, but we didn't want to carry fuel up six flights of stairs,' says Andre. 'It's hard to get gas fireplaces in France, so we imported this one from England.' It was set off-centre, which fits in perfectly with the unit's sweeping curve. The central pod connects everything else, and oddly, although it is so large, and dominates the apartment, it conveys a sense of spaciousness. As Andre says, 'In a small apartment, you need a feeling of space, and being able to walk three metres without bumping into something at once makes you feel that you are in a large area.'

Although the apartment had to be almost completely gutted, they managed to preserve and restore the old wooden floor in the bedroom. The rest of the floor had to be taken up, so it was decided to install a concrete floor, in keeping with the new look of the apartment. There are, however, practical problems about making a concrete floor in a sixth-floor flat. It is not at all easy – actually, it is very difficult – to get such things as a concrete polishing machine onto the site. They found a pragmatic solution. The decorator created 'a sauce' of pigments and the apartment now has an interestingly coloured, poured-concrete, matt floor, which requires no rugs and which contrasts well with the high shine of the bright red lacquered pod.

Since the pod is so modern, it accentuates period features such as the exposed beams and the wooden floor. This matters a lot to Marianne. 'When you are doing an apartment, you ought to keep the spirit of the building,' she says. 'Architecture is a layer of things, and a well-designed apartment should look as if it is of its own place. I see apartments that look as though they could be anywhere – Tokyo, New York, London – but I think that they should look as if they are where they are.' Andre, meanwhile, feels very positive about his new Paris base: 'I take great pleasure in the fact that things are where I expect them to be. I love this flat. It is warm, light and cosy – everything we want, in fact.'

left Facing the bedroom, framed by beams, is a bathroom that is accessed from a flat panelled door in the central pod.

right On the other side of the pod, to the left of the fireplace, Marianne Pascal managed to squeeze a tiny but extremely useful, shower room out of the available space.

this page For such a small space, the main bathroom is surprisingly commodious -- not to say, luxurious. having not only a full-sized bath but also a basin unit and ample room for the storage of towels and bathroom bottles.

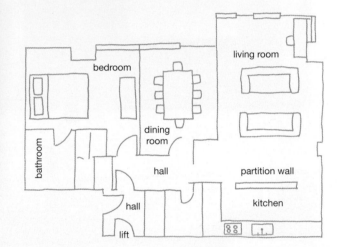

bedroom

living room

dining room

bathroom

hall

hall

partition wall

kitchen

lift

above In the entrance to the apartment, the attention is caught by an antique chest on the far wall of the living area. The arrangement of objects on top of the chest, including a painting by Howard Hodgkin, make a point of immediate interest.

INDUSTRIAL CHIC

The dress designer Jacques Azagury is a newcomer to apartment living. His previous home was a Georgian house, which he gave up because he disliked having to run up and down the stairs all the time. His new apartment, in an old industrial building in Covent Garden, is reached by a lift.

this page The long, narrow living space is balanced by the ceiling-high windows, the potential monotony of which has been broken up by the use of glass bricks in one panel as well as the sliding fabric screens, which were installed instead of curtains or blinds.

this picture At one end of the living area, Jacques has created a compact work space that is separate from, but easily absorbed into, the central area.

this picture The partition wall hides most of the workings of the kitchen, but the mirror on the far wall, behind the units, bounces light from the window back into the room.

above The simple kitchen, behind the partition wall, has units on both sides and, at one end, an eye-level oven.

- ❏ **The lines of every piece of furniture in this apartment are very clean and rectangular, so they all harmonize.**

- ❏ **The glass window bricks add a decorative touch as well as cleverly fulfilling a practical purpose, letting light in while giving privacy to the working end of the living room.**

- ❏ **A simple partition wall with egress at both ends is an easy solution to the problem of the integral kitchen.**

One reason why Jacques Azagury chose this particular apartment was that he did not have too many adjustments to make to it. When he found it, it was light, well laid out and easy to manage – almost an equation for the perfect apartment. What it did require, though, were those subtle adjustments that make the difference between the everyday and the outstanding – or high street and couture, to make the analogy a little more personal.

Jacques did, however, make two major changes. He put in pale-toned wood flooring throughout the flat (other than in the bedroom) and installed underfloor heating – something that is often well worth doing in an apartment if you are already doing some major structural work, since it frees up valuable wall and floor space. Although the colour of the floor seems perfect, reflecting daylight and generally enlarging the whole area, it was not actually the colour that Jacques wanted. He had originally chosen a darker tone, but a mistake was made by the installers and the finished shade was much lighter. It was a serendipitous accident, and today he much prefers his light, subtle floor.

The other major change, and one that now defines the apartment, was Jacques's decision to erect a partial wall between the kitchen end of the apartment and the rest of the living room. Like all the best ideas, it seems so simple: the paraphernalia of

this page Although it may seem a surprising use of space, Jacques regards a separate dining room as worth more than its keep. He is a man who, when he entertains, likes to do it properly.

cooking is hidden away from the rest of the room, while light is brought into the kitchen, and the proportions of the room are not reduced as they would have been had the entire kitchen area been cut off. Indeed, the proportions and scale of the room are in some senses enhanced since the frameless openings into the kitchen add to the varied geometric pleasures of the space.

At one end of the kitchen wall, facing the rest of the room through the opening, Jacques hung a mirror. 'I did it to extend the space,' he explains, 'and also to reflect the light from the tall windows at the far end of the apartment.'

There is a ceiling-height, metal-framed wall of glass, part of which consists of a set of sliding glass doors and the other part of glass bricks, which continue round the corner to give light to Jacques's desk. Instead of curtains, Jacques has installed opaque fabric panels, made of stiffened blind material, which slide on runners across the window. Against the dark frames of the window panes, the effect is distinctly Oriental.

'I don't like colour,' he says and indeed, throughout the apartment, there is little extra colour apart from the odd, striking vase of flowers. But this is the sort of apartment in which colour is not needed – from the pale limed floor to the plain carpet rug and the simple matching cream sofas, it is a calm place in which the different textures and tones are highlighted by copious natural light, as well as the subtle additional lighting, particularly the downlighters that are used throughout the apartment.

The other rooms are subtle rather than statement-making. Unusually, Jacques has designed one room as a dining room rather than the more usual second bedroom/study combination. Its Zen-like ambience fits in with the overall tranquillity of both texture and tone – an example of east-meets-west at its best.

above There is very little furniture in the bedroom. A classic double chest of drawers at one end provides flexible storage and blends in with the overall, pared-back style of the room.

below The bedroom leads into a shower room. Jacques's predilection for art and objects placed at unconventional heights is exemplified by the mirror resting at an angle against the wall.

OPEN PLANS

Lars Kristensen, owner of the fashionable antiques shop Fildefer in Copenhagen, has created his perfect home on the top floor of a 19th-century apartment building in the Frederickersberg quarter of the city.

Lars Kristensen's home in Copenhagen is not a conversion but part of a 19th-century purpose-built apartment block. When Lars bought the apartment, in 1998, it had been lived in by the same family for the preceding thirty years. The walk-up apartment is typically Danish in the way that the main reception rooms run along the front and a long corridor links these rooms and the bedrooms at the back with the kitchen and what would once have been the service quarters at the far end, away from the rest of the living accommodation.

left Lars places everything with great care and precision. Here, in the living area, he has arranged a composition of objects and art on a long pier table.

this page The living room is a combination of comfort and classicism. On the far wall, a striking work by Maibritt Ulvedal-Bjelke injects colour into what is otherwise a neutral palette with nothing to disturb the neutral, calm tones of furniture, walls and floor.

Lars acquired the apartment in a hurry. Having viewed it only once, he bought it overnight, after leaving a phone message to say that he wanted to take it. When he went to visit the apartment again, he noticed how dark it was, with lowered ceilings and the glassed parts of the internal doors boarded over, but he could also see that it had potential. Although the interior was apparently so dark, its position on the top floor of the building meant that it could receive maximum natural light from three sides – the building is on a corner, and looks over a school playground to the rear.

Nevertheless, the apartment as a whole felt as closed up as a parcel. 'I knew that I would have to unwrap it to get down to the real thing, and I wasn't sure what I'd find when I got there,' says Lars. 'I couldn't see what might be within. So I acquired it rapidly but, since I didn't have the money to do it all at once, I then had to assemble it slowly.'

The first rooms that he attacked were the living areas, his office and his bedroom. 'There were three painters here for a month, peeling off ten layers of wall and ceiling paper, removing the boards from the glass sections of the internal doors, as well as

this picture This room combines the new, the old and the serendipitous finds such as the industrial metal cabinet in the corner that Lars discovered in a shipyard and which now houses all the audio equipment. Decking it with candlesticks and lights makes the cabinet's origins hard to identify.

left Chairs are draped with linen sheets and throughout the room are quirky pieces found by Lars such as the model of a theatre interior, formerly used by hotel concierges to indicate the position of seats to possible patrons.

this picture From the dining room there are views through to the sitting room and to the central corridor with Lars's office beyond. Although there is a sense of space, there is also an easy and logical flow between the different areas and a fluent coherence in the interior design.

this picture Displaying a quirky and comfortable taste, Lars has combined any number of styles and periods to harmonious and undeniably Scandinavian effect, from the 18th-century dining table to the 20th-century metal prison or hospital chairs.

restoring and lightening the floors.' The pine floors had originally been heavily varnished. Lars stripped them and whitewashed them. There are no rugs in the apartment – he doesn't need them or see the point of them.

To open up the apartment further, Lars removed the door between the hall and the dining room, and then created visual links between the dining room and the living room beyond it. To lead the eye onwards, he painted the two rooms in similar tones. Although some might think it unusual today to have a separate dining room, in Lars's hands it is not a closed-off, isolated sort of room but very much part of the general living area. As he says, 'It doesn't feel cut off from the rest of the apartment and if – as I do – you have twelve people to dinner five times a year, then it is worth having; indeed, it's very nice to have.'

On the right of the corridor is his office, 'the centre of the apartment', from where one can see in several directions at once, and which leads into the bedroom – which originally had four

this page The final part of the apartment to be converted by Lars, the kitchen was created out of three small, irregular rooms that included the servants' quarters. It is now a large working and dining kitchen in which the cooking and utility area is concentrated at one end of the room, with a simple breakfast table at the other. The two are linked by a decorative painted table against the wall.

right The dark, narrow hall is typical of old Danish apartment buildings of this age. Layers of paper were removed from the glass panels above the doors to bring some much needed light into the centre of the space.

below The bathroom can accommodate only a shower and a basin, but it is well designed in that it has all that is needed in exactly the right place.

doors leading off it, until Lars closed off one. The bedroom itself is neat, clean and rather functional; to Lars, it has a more modern feeling about it. One door leads into the small bathroom, which Lars tackled three years after the first renovation, and which is now bereft of its gaudy orange and brown tiles, finished instead with all-white ones. This room is a good example of Lars's enduring need to match the functional with the aesthetic. 'While aesthetics are important to me, I realize that we need functional things to sustain ordinary life,' he says. 'I have to shower and wash, for example – but I would still rather have a good-looking shower, and even if it does splash water a bit, I would rather dry the floor than have an ugly shower.'

What is now the kitchen was, when he found the flat, three rooms, one of them a maid's room and furnished with a stove in the corner. Now it is a pleasing, light room with angles, one end devoted to the mechanics of cooking and cleaning, the other to the pleasures of dining, with a small, old table and chairs and a bench in the window.

Many of the objects in the apartment are antique, while the artworks are modern. 'I like the mixture,' says Lars. 'In the dining room is a chandelier from a Swedish castle, an 18th-century wooden table and 20th-century metal chairs, originally made for prison use.' Lars looks out for objects that combine function and decoration – in the sitting room, a metal cabinet that he found in a shipyard houses all the stereo equipment. All the furnishings are simple and there are few curtains; some chairs are covered with simple ticking, others with white linen sheets. It's an interesting

❏ **Old and new furniture can be mixed together as long as the different proportions and scale are taken into account when placing the pieces.**

❏ **Lars Kristensen shows very effectively how to combine industrial pieces of furniture with more domesticated designs.**

❏ **In every room there are small, decorative details that show up the purity of the overall design.**

mixture, but one that appears deceptively simple – in reality, it is a difficult look to achieve and it's hard to create the right juxtaposition of hard and soft.

The colours used in the decoration of the apartment are equally low-key. 'Copenhagen doesn't have much light so you need to add as much as you can through the walls,' says Lars. 'I always go for soft-washed colours, including light grey. I like a contrast between the walls and the much stronger colours of the artworks. It's a sort of mixture of Swedish and French with a touch of English.'

From Lars's point of view, his home represents perfection. 'For my way of life, I need a retreat from the fuss and noise of the street, so I must have around me a few, well-chosen things. What I enjoy is the architectural feeling of the apartment, and the knowledge that I didn't need to add much to the original.'

above left The bedroom's simple furniture includes a cupboard that Lars found in his grandfather's garage, a wooden table furnished with pots of herbs and a mirror positioned to one side of the table.

above Something of a corridor until Lars closed off one of the three doors leading into it, the bedroom still opens directly into the study. On the wall opposite the bed is a batik by Claude Viallat.

2
SPLIT-LEVEL
APARTMENTS

HAVEN IN MINIATURE

Paris, a city that constantly and pleasantly surprises, is full of secret spaces. In the sixième arrondisement, amid gracious and elegant buildings, is this hidden gem.

One of the many talents of the French architect Marianne Pascal is her ability to fashion something special from seemingly uninspiring spaces such as this tiny dwelling, a real *sous-les-toits de Paris* sort of place. Here, Marianne has created a cosy split-level apartment that combines everything including the kitchen sink in the smallest of spaces. Outside the living room, a tiny terrace is filled with plants and shrubs as well as a table, long bench and chairs. Provence is evoked by the mimosa and Mediterranean pine tree that, rather amazingly, grow in pots. The windows that open onto the terrace have sheer curtains that diffuse the surprisingly bright light; these are hung on hinged rods attached to the windows that swing back and allow the windows to open inwards.

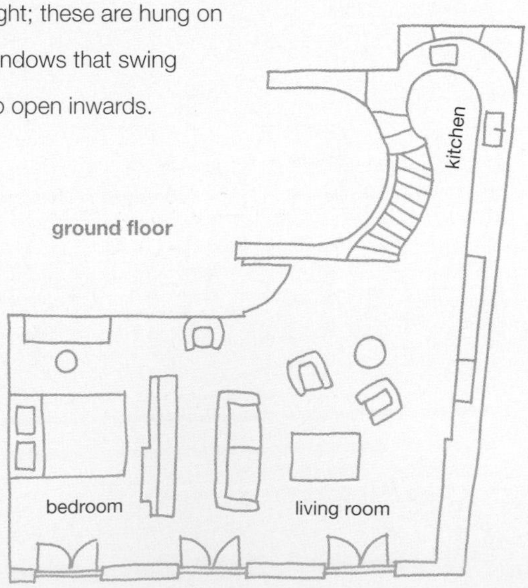

ground floor

kitchen

opposite This tiny apartment has been so artfully designed that the living area, with its central focus of an open, log-burning fire, far from appearing small, gives off an air of spacious comfort.

bedroom

living room

below The total living area is divided by a partition wall that effectively breaks the area into two, while allowing easy access to both sides.

right The partition wall is in fact a subtly designed storage space, with a low-level unit on one side that also acts as a display surface and, on the other, full-height open storage for books and discs.

From the moment you enter the apartment it is clear that not an inch of space has been wasted. The ground-floor living area is divided by a half-wall, on one side of which is a pretty, commodious sitting space that includes a traditional fireplace and two comfortable chairs; on the other side is a space that can be used as part of the main room at a gathering but which also fills several other functions, including spare room, study and television room.

The room divider is a two-way storage unit. On the sitting-room side, the unit is low enough to provide a surface for lamps and the display of artworks; at the window end, a narrow, ceiling-high, closed shelf unit holds books. On the other side, the divider becomes an open shelving unit with space for books, pictures and CDs.

It was always going to be hard to find a place for a kitchen in this little space, but no Paris apartment can be without somewhere to cook. Marianne's clever idea was to carve out from behind, and almost beneath, the staircase a semicircular space, like a ship's galley, in which every centimetre is put to good use.

Since there is no natural light in this cubby-hole kitchen, artificial light, provided by a daylight bulb, shines from behind a panel. Everything is tucked away – there is even storage in what looks, at first glance, like the service duct. The units are panelled in wood, as are the cupboards that run along the fireplace wall in the living room; a narrow strip of ebonized wood connects the two.

The remainder of the space tells the same story. When it comes to devising storage, not a single square centimetre has been ignored. It is not just a matter of the ordinary solutions, such as the tall cupboards running right to the rear of the living room, but also the less obvious ideas such as cupboards cunningly built into the side of the staircase,

a tall unit that conceals drawers and cupboards, and even a narrow alcove running to the rear of the room that has enough space for glasses to be stored in single lines. None of the ideas is at all complicated; in fact, many of them are common sense. It's simply that they have been implemented rather than just thought about!

The bedroom and bathing area is reached by going up the open staircase. At the top of the steps is a tiny, angular shower room and lavatory, the space even more ship-like than the kitchen below. Around the corner, past a set of

above An open staircase leads to the bedroom. To have enclosed it would have broken up the space. Behind it is a tiny kitchen, tucked into an alcove.

left The living room and kitchen storage are aesthetically linked by a single line of ebonized wood that runs the length of the wall from the fireplace to the kitchen.

book shelves, comes a surprise: a bath encased in an oak surround that, on the wall side, follows the irregular angles of this attic room. On the outer side of the bath, however, the oak casing curves outwards, like a sturdy boat, towards the confident curves of the storage unit opposite, whose shape is an equally successful wooden variation of the curved laminate pod that Marianne designed for Andre Cohen (see pages 62–69). The irregular, uneven planes of this attic are forgotten, and we remember only Marianne Pascal's clever design, in this smallest of split-level spaces.

❑ **Lateral thinking, like lateral planning, can make a split-level apartment out of the most unpromising of spaces.**

❑ **On the upper level, rather than scale down, the architect has scaled up with her dramatic bath design.**

❑ **Throughout the space, both upstairs and down, every inch has been used, every corner and wall has a purpose.**

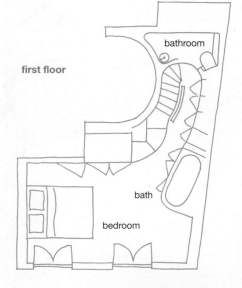

first floor

bathroom

bath

bedroom

left The upper floor, under the eaves, now houses a shower room and a bedroom, with the bath centre stage. All are connected by a curving, wooden storage space.

right The smallest of shower rooms, angled to make the maximum use of space, is set directly above the stairs.

opposite Clad in wood, the lidded bath sweeps round the bedroom edge, its curves echoed by the facing cupboards.

this picture In this classic London apartment, on the ground floor of a well-proportioned 19th-century house, John and Florence Pearse have used the space wisely, allowing generous spacing between the pieces of furniture.

MODERN CLASSIC

Originally two separate units – a two-room ground-floor flat and a small first-floor studio – this living space has been converted into a one-bedroom split-level apartment of great charm.

John and Florence Pearse designed and decorated this apartment in a mid-19th century, stucco-clad London building 15 years ago, and it is a measure of the thought and intelligence that went into the planning and choice of furnishings that the apartment looks as fresh, modern and interesting today as it did then. John Pearse calls himself a classical modernist – not a bad description, although modern classicist might have done equally well. He is patently not an advocate of change for the sake of change, and each item of furniture, each element, has been chosen with care and deliberation.

right A narrow internal hall means that the Pearses were able to make a door that opened directly into the sitting room, while retaining the original double-door space that leads through to the kitchen beyond.

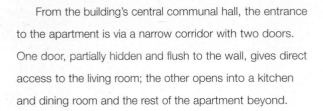

this picture The long, narrow table can be folded in on itself to provide a wider, squarer surface. This is a sophisticated solution to the kitchen table/dining table conundrum that is so often encountered in open living spaces. The chairs are a Philippe Starck design called Louis XX.

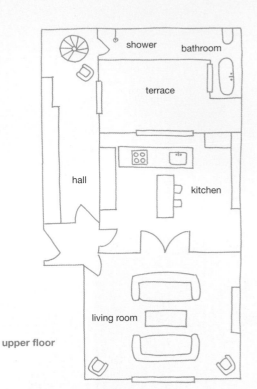

upper floor

shower

bathroom

terrace

hall

kitchen

living room

From the building's central communal hall, the entrance to the apartment is via a narrow corridor with two doors. One door, partially hidden and flush to the wall, gives direct access to the living room; the other opens into a kitchen and dining room and the rest of the apartment beyond.

The Pearses installed double doors between the living room and the kitchen; when the doors are open, the effect is to extend the available space and light. On either side of the double doors are two wall-hung open-shelf units, fixed a small distance above the skirting to give the impression that they are free-floating; the books are arranged in a seemingly haphazard way, although in truth there is nothing haphazard about their arrangement at all – like everything else, their placing has been carefully thought out. Apart from this installation, there is no built-in furniture and the pieces that are there, such as the sofa from Florence's childhood

this picture Although the wooden rack beyond the sink looks as if it might hold wine bottles, it is in fact a door that conceals the washing machine, ironing board and other essential equipment.

this page John and Florence Pearse installed, in the 1990s, a semi-mobile kitchen made by Bulthaup that consists of a hob, oven and sink in one flexible, unfitted unit. Fifteen years on, the design still looks impressive.

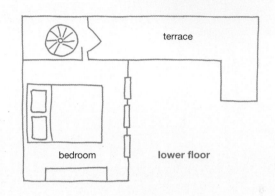

terrace

bedroom   **lower floor**

home, are graceful and light in appearance. One unexpected element is that the walls are covered in anaglypta – a wall covering more closely associated with old-fashioned Indian restaurants than with design purists, but here it has been treated with several layers of matt white paint, giving it a textural depth and the appearance of old panels of embossed leather or antique textiles.

The kitchen is as open and simple as the living area. Chairs designed by Phillipe Starck surround a refectory-style table that folds in half horizontally. At the window end of the room is a mobile kitchen by Bulthaup, consisting of a stainless-steel oven, range and sink in one seamless unit – a design that looks as innovative and interesting as it did when it was first introduced, and which has clearly proved its worth; 15 years later, it is as striking and practical as it ever was.

The storage in the kitchen is simple, deceptive and unobtrusive. Perhaps the wittiest touch is at one side of the window: what at first appears to be wooden wine storage unit is in fact the door to a store-all cupboard, holding everything from ironing board to washing machine, as well as all the other paraphernalia that even the most purist design-lover needs.

Like everything else, storage has been well thought out. The linking corridor that leads to the rear of the apartment is a wall of storage that uses the space beneath the main staircase of the house to create a small lavatory as well as an all-embracing little cloakroom with shelving and plenty of hanging space.

Beyond the cloakroom, the corridor widens slightly, and there John and Florence have carved out a space that

above At the end of the corridor, a spiral staircase leads upstairs; opposite, a glass door opens into the L-shaped bathroom, where you step directly into the shower area.

above left In the corridor linking the main rooms with the staircase up to the bedroom, a clothes storage area has been combined with a built-in desk unit, complete with shelves and hidden doors for books and office equipment.

this page The short arm of the L-shaped room is entirely filled by a luxurious bath with an alcove at one end for towels and a glass wall divided into compartments that are deep enough to hold bottles and pots.

- ❏ **The Pearses have proved that classically designed pieces – if well selected and placed – will always look good.**

- ❏ **Storage has been very carefully thought out and every corner has been brilliantly used.**

- ❏ **Glass is cleverly used on every level, especially in the bathroom, where both frosted and clear glass greatly add to the design.**

left and right The compact but comfortable bedroom, reached by a spiral staircase, has been carved out of what was once a separate studio space. Facing the top of the stairs, a door opens onto a small terrace, above the bathroom, which is deep enough to hold a table and chairs. Inside, the rest of the space is taken up by the bed and a panelled wood surround, part of which conceals extra storage.

not only holds a wardrobe and shelves for clothes but also acts as a study, with a cleverly designed built-in desk surrounded by bookshelves. At the rear of the space, leading to the bedroom above, is a spiral staircase. Throughout the apartment the Pearses have used the same pale wood floor, sealed with a reflective finish, that enhances the sense of light in every room.

To the right, opposite the staircase – in an innovative and artful use of space – a bathroom has been carved out of what was previously a dead area containing the apartment's original well, which had been filled in by the Pearses. A smoked-glass door opens directly into a shower room that runs parallel to the back wall of the building. At the far end are a basin and lavatory and, at right angles, parallel to the study space and running along the opposite side of the well, is a long deep bath; its outside wall is divided into squares of frosted glass, deeply set to create niches for the storage of creams and unguents.

At the top of the spiral staircase is a minute bedroom containing virtually nothing apart from the bed and yet more storage space, concealed behind wooden panels. On the roof of the shower room beneath, Florence has created a pleasant terrace complete with pots and plants.

The care that the Pearses have taken in every last detail illustrates one of the first lessons of apartment living: if you want to get it right, think everything through – from spaces to storage – right from the beginning. It's a discipline, and it's necessary.

this page A living area where doors have been removed and walls brought down makes for the maximum use of all available space. A beautiful oak floor runs through the apartment and a sofa against the wall connects the kitchen at the back to the eating and working zone at the front.

SIMPLY SUBTLE

This light-filled apartment was once divided up into many small rooms – until architect and designer Signe Henriksen came along and knocked down most of the internal walls.

The apartment that Signe Bindslev Henriksen has designed for herself and her two-year-old son is notable for the feeling of space, light and total flexibility that she has managed to achieve. It is a fascinating study in the use of space. Signe's home is carved out of the upper floors of an old house on the edge of Copenhagen; originally built for the farmers who then worked there, the houses in this district were divided into many rooms – about three on every floor, each floor housing one family. Not unnaturally, the first thing Signe did was to take down all the doors and most of the walls. 'I wanted to make one space on each floor,' she says. 'I didn't need doors because with two floors I already have a natural barrier between the different parts of the house. The first floor was to be the living area, and the top floor the bedroom. I also needed space on the floor for my son to play.'

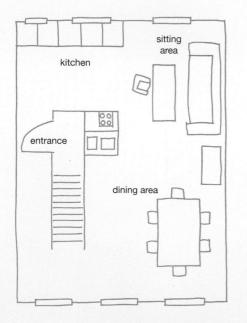

above right Next to the long table, a mirror reflects the view all the way back to the other end of the apartment, showing the staircase that leads up to the bedroom.

right There is little decoration for decoration's sake in this restrained apartment, but the decorative objects that are there have been chosen with care.

ground floor

left Making good use of the architectural and structural features, the cooker has been set back in a niche in the corner wall that partially divides the kitchen from the rest of the apartment.

right The main run of kitchen units, made in MDF, was designed by Signe, as was the leather-seated stool. All the elements are deliberately understated in tone, in common with the rest of the furniture in the apartment.

right, inset Visible from the kitchen are the sofa and low table, also designed by Signe, in the area where guests gather before dinner.

Today, when you enter the apartment you find a wall directly in front of you. A turn to the left takes you to the front of the house and into the living area; a turn to the right takes you into the long kitchen space that runs along the back of the apartment before turning back on itself to lead into the living area from the other side. The absence of doorways is irrelevant. Signe uses existing angles and corners to lead the eye and to hide what is necessary to keep out of sight.

The kitchen was originally about half its present length. After some internal demolition, Signe installed units down most of the length of the back wall, using a partial wall to screen the cooker and the refrigerator from view. At the far end, a sofa against the party wall metaphorically turns the corner out of the kitchen and seamlessly marks the transition into the living area, which is dominated by a long dining/work table and chairs on silent castors. The partial wall serves to conceal the fridge and, indeed, the whole kitchen from anyone sitting at the table; it is remarkable that the apparatus of kitchen life is hidden away without there being any sense of anything closed off at all.

When an apartment consists basically of a single space, and there are no door frames or other floor-level distractions, the flooring takes on particular importance because it facilitates the flow through the area. In this case, the flooring, carefully chosen by Signe, consists of oak boards 3 mm thick from Dinesen. Signe designed much of the furniture in the apartment,

including the coffee table and the long dining table, and gave much thought to what else she wanted in the space. 'I've mixed together pieces of furniture, including some pieces that I inherited from my grandmother,' she explains.

Signe instinctively knows what she likes and doesn't like, and is confident in her own style. 'I'm not actually into a certain style. For me, it's important that furniture should be beautiful but it doesn't matter what period or place a piece is from. I don't think that it's difficult to combine, say, chrome and oak, as long as the background is well thought out and right.' She prefers to choose materials in understated

this page The stairs, which have been opened up to become an integral part of the apartment, lead to the open-plan bedroom above, with the bathroom situated at the top of the stairs.

colours, with oak as the wood of preference. 'When you have relatively low ceilings, it's better to have pale colours or neutrals. If you introduce colour, everything else is drawn to it – it would be the central focus – and in a small space you don't want that. It is one of the reasons why I have no curtains in the apartment. It is simply too small for curtains; they become a piece of furniture that takes up part of my floor space. I don't have carpets either, for the same reason.'

Upstairs was originally a hallway with two rooms leading from it – all with fairly low ceilings. 'There was quite a lot of unused roof space, so my idea was to open it up as much

below At the top of the stairs is a cubed unit that is used to store linen. Some linen is stacked in the cubes; the rest is stored in baskets. The bathroom is immediately adjacent.

right The area to the left of the stairs has been opened up and on the far wall is a collection of paintings by Vincent, Signe's two-year-old son, including *Panda in the Forest*.

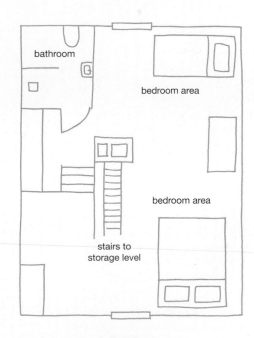

first floor

as I could and make it a completely flexible space. I wanted to create a small bathroom, one very large sleeping area, as well as storage, and a small, easily accessible attic area where I could keep all my books and things that I don't need on a daily basis.'

The first thing she did was to open up the roof and install sloping windows. At the top of the stairs is open storage for linen, next to the bathroom. To the right is one light-filled room that, since it is open to the rafters, feels immensely spacious. Beneath the new windows is a child's bed and on the other side of the room, under the other new window, is another, larger bed. Round to the right, in the space over the corridor below, is a large curtained-off enclosure with hanging and stacking storage, and running up one side of this is a wooden set of steps leading to the extra storage space directly beneath the eaves.

'When I moved in, I got rid of over half of my things,' says Signe. 'I don't have a nostalgic feeling about possessions, and I change pictures and things around a lot – which I why I keep pictures against the wall. It could look completely different in six months' time. We live in a detox life – to feel right, you just have to get rid of the unimportant stuff.' Which is perhaps a lesson that many of us could learn from!

❑ **The work done in the upper half of this small house was radical but has resulted in a split-level space that seems much larger than it really is.**

❑ **One enormous bedroom combined with a playroom at the top of the house is an original, inspired idea.**

❑ **Taking out the doors and using the inner architecture, such as corners and piers, to define different areas has greatly simplified the design.**

FAMILY FRIENDLY

This maisonette on the two upper floors of a town house is arranged with a staircase leading from the front door to the living area on the first floor, from where a further flight leads to the bedrooms above.

There are as many different ways to arrange an apartment as there ways actually to live in one. One route is to make major structural and decorative changes and to reconfigure totally the space, changing it into something new. Another option is to go along with what already exists and change your way of life to suit the space. A third, perhaps the most practical option, is to make a few changes and, with those as your starting point, concentrate on the important personal and particular details that will make the space your own, and one that will suit every member of the family.

Kamilla Byriel and Christian Permin, have taken the pragmatic route. Their apartment is light, bright and peaceful; it is hard to believe that it is home not only to Kamilla and Christian but also to their three small children. Under different circumstances, it might be a mess; amazingly, it is calm and well ordered. That is not because Kamilla is a controlling sort of woman, but simply because she and Christian have thought logically about the space available and decided to take what is there and make it work for them in the most comfortable way they can. Kamilla is part of a innovative clothing company, Stella Nova, which is perhaps where her design and organizational abilities have been honed.

One of the first, and possibly simplest, decisions Kamilla and Christian made was that child-life would take place on the upper floor of the apartment, with each of the children's bedrooms becoming a combination of play and bedroom. It is cheerful and

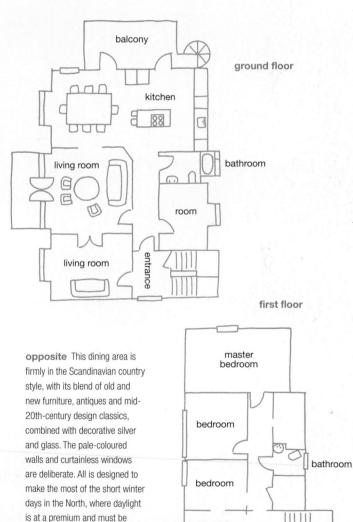

opposite This dining area is firmly in the Scandinavian country style, with its blend of old and new furniture, antiques and mid-20th-century design classics, combined with decorative silver and glass. The pale-coloured walls and curtainless windows are deliberate. All is designed to make the most of the short winter days in the North, where daylight is at a premium and must be seized whenever possible.

this picture While the other end of this long, light-filled room is designed for dining, this end is devoted to kitchen life. Set against the wall is a simple range of storage units and the sink; in front of that, an island unit doubles as a food-preparation and cooking area, holding the hob, and a breakfast bar.

this picture Although partly a working kitchen, this room is above all the heart of the home. Everywhere there are small decorative touches, such as this table with two posters on and above it, as well as pieces of china and glass.

this picture Among the most useful of all kitchen furniture items is the island unit with more than one function. This one not only has an inset hob but also holds saucepans tidily and conveniently below. The worktop extends beyond the hob area to make a sitting spot.

left The antique wooden work table that is used as a dining table can seat at least eight people and is set with an ever-changing selection of chairs, some old wooden ones, some moulded plastic.

right From the kitchen there is a view into the central living room and the small room beyond. The rug here is the only concession to floor coverings. Elsewhere, the white-gloss-painted floor flows from space to space.

messy up there, but the arrangement work because it means that downstairs is relatively clutter-free, calm and friendly – not a child-free zone by any means, for the children are most welcome downstairs and spend most of their time there; it is rather that all the paraphernalia of childhood is kept not only out of sight but also in a place of its own.

The living floor consists of two rooms that run into each other, with at one end a kitchen that extends across the whole width of the house. When Kamilla and Christian moved in, the middle room, rather than being a living space, was a wide hall that led to the kitchen in one direction and the small living room in the other. They closed up the doors into the hall from the corridor, creating a large extra living space that linked one end of the apartment with the other. The middle room is now a family room complete with a sofa that is large enough to seat the whole family at once.

The long kitchen is the hub of the apartment. At one end, a wide window provides light for the old wooden work table used as a dining table; at the other end, there is an all-white kitchen area with an island unit, containing the hob and saucepan storage, and a sink unit against the wall. As in the rest of the apartment, the floors have been painted high-shine white; the ceilings and walls are also white. Scandinavian winters can be long and the days short, so there is an instinctive desire among Scandinavians to catch as much of the fleeting light as possible.

Since Kamilla and Christian had decided against major structural work, they knew that it was the details that would make the apartment theirs – in particular, the carefully

this page In the central living room is a pair of wicker PK 22 chairs by Poul Kjäerholm defined by another wicker piece that looks like an oversized bottle gourd. Beneath the window is a workman's bench used as a table with an arrangement of candlesticks and flowers used in decorative juxtaposition.

right The view along the length of the apartment from the far room into the kitchen shows that space flow need not be hard to arrange. Here, merely closing off the door from the hall made this space a comfortable room as well as an area that leads the eye easily from one end to the other.

- ❏ **The Byriels are living proof that it *is* possible to combine a pleasant, attractive apartment with three young children.**

- ❏ **They opted for a solution that is simple but effective: the majority of child-oriented objects are stored in each child's room on the upper floor.**

- ❏ **The mixture of old and new, different periods and materials is well thought out in these living rooms.**

- ❏ **Closing off the door that led from the corridor into the middle room has completely altered the living space available.**

chosen furniture and the placing of objects. The couple are proud of their Scandinavian design heritage, and the furniture in the apartment ranges from 19th-century family pieces to iconic, recognizable pieces from the 20th century. In the kitchen, for example, is an antique, glass-fronted cupboard inherited by Kamilla, and lights by Verner Panton, while in the far sitting room is the open-leaf-shape, black leather chair designed by Arne Jacobsen. 'You can use his pieces anywhere in a house,' says Kamilla. 'If you have a few basic pieces, they can go with you through your life, and each piece of furniture here has its own story, something which is very important to us.' The way it is

combined is also important. As Kamilla says, 'It's all to do with the mix,' which means combining the modern and the antique in clever and unusual ways.

There are no curtains in the apartment, nor, except in the middle room, are there any rugs. It might be thought that this lack of furnishings would make the space rather cold, but, on the contrary, it is as warm and welcoming as if it were hung with textiles from ceiling to floor. This is the effect Kamilla wanted to achieve for, as she says, 'The weather here is not very nice and we spend a lot of time indoors, so it's important to us to have somewhere that is comfortable, functional and personal too.'

3 LOFTS & LARGE APARTMENTS

LATERAL LOGIC

William and Trine Miller and their two small daughters live in a large, laterally converted flat that runs over the first floors of two classic stucco houses in central London.

By the time the Millers bought the property, the adjacent flats had already been converted into one large living space, but the two main reception rooms were separate from each other, accessible only by a central corridor. What is now the kitchen was the sitting room, and the present drawing room was divided into a bedroom, a bathroom and an extra little bit. The original kitchen was in what is now the girls' bedroom, and the main bedroom and bathroom area were very different. It was obvious that, if possible, the two reception rooms should be restored to their former prominence. 'I wanted to reinstate them even at the cost of losing an extra

above and opposite The sitting end of the large living space is decorated in a style and colours that sit comfortably with the kitchen beyond, as the two are connected by an imposing pair of double doors that are usually left wide open. Small design details such as the loose covers on the dining chairs help to pull the rooms together.

above It is hard to believe that everything in this room was newly installed by Trine Miller. By concentrating on the scale and proportion of furniture and architecture, she has ensured that the room has a classic, timeless look that makes it seem both old and new at the same time.

bedroom,' says Trine. 'These buildings were meant to have fine reception rooms and I knew that we could use them properly.' So William and Trine decided to use the two principal rooms – which would originally have been two separate drawing rooms – as an interconnecting space, with the kitchen at one end, the drawing room at the other, and the two linked by a pair of double doors.

Although the decision might have been seen as not entirely conventional – many would have installed the kitchen in one of the smaller areas perhaps, rather than giving it such a dominant role – the final result is a resounding triumph. Since the two rooms flow, via the double doors, one into the other and yet have entirely separate functions,

there is a feeling of ease and space that might otherwise be missing. The sense of flow is also emphasized by the floor coverings chosen by Trine. 'In many apartments, you are restricted by the lease as to what type of floors you can have. The kitchen and bathroom can have hard flooring, but not the other rooms, so in those we laid sea grass, which has a similar appearance to a wooden floor, and we put all the heating under the floor. This is much more convenient than conventional radiatiors, which take up wall space, as well as allowing the heat to rise to the ceiling.'

Although the kitchen seems very large, the floor area is actually smaller than it was originally. Trine built inwards from the inner wall to make a floor-to-ceiling wall of storage,

above and top When a kitchen is used for eating as well as cooking – and leads into a sitting area – the arrangement and storage of utensils and equipment should be both tidy and decorative: not always an easy balance.

above left By confining the cooking area to the far wall, Trine has ensured that the table becomes an inviting place for guests to sit down and eat; machine-washable chair covers add to the comfortable air.

this picture This wall of flush doors is more complex than it seems. While the open door is indeed a door and leads into the hall, behind all the other doors is stored all kinds of kitchen paraphernalia, including the washing machine and dryer. The run of cupboards is broken only by a large stainless-steel refrigerator.

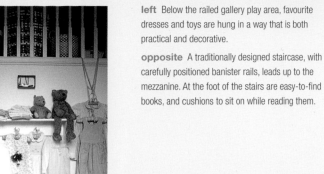

left Below the railed gallery play area, favourite dresses and toys are hung in a way that is both practical and decorative.

opposite A traditionally designed staircase, with carefully positioned banister rails, leads up to the mezzanine. At the foot of the stairs are easy-to-find books, and cushions to sit on while reading them.

below The Millers' two young daughters have bunk beds in their room at the far end of the apartment, which has a bathroom next to it. The ceiling was very high – too high, in fact – so Trine decided to make the most of the space by putting in a small mezzanine floor that is designed as a children's playroom, with plenty of room for storage.

accommodating a full-height cupboard as well as a washing machine and dryer and a large fridge-freezer. The floor space is still big enough for a wall of kitchen units, a large dining table and chairs, a two-seater sofa and a small play table and chairs for the girls. The use of space reflects Trine's priorities. 'If you don't have a room where you can store things, then you must be able to store them behind doors on different levels. We're lucky here in that the ceilings are so high – actually, in some areas, such as the children's room, too high. To get the proportions right, we lowered the ceilings, allowing us to make two attic spaces for storage.'

The girls' room is at the kitchen end of the apartment with an adjoining bathroom. The high ceiling in their room had another advantage, for it was there that Trine designed a mezzanine gallery, which is reached from the lower part of the room

above If a bathroom is big enough, nothing is more luxurious or comfortable than a well-upholstered armchair that can be used to sit on while chatting or reading.

left Separated from the main public areas by a door, the main bedroom has been designed as a simple and uncluttered space. As the clothes storage is outside, this room is a wholly tranquil sleeping spot.

by a short staircase. Kitted out in best Wendy House style, it makes a permanent playroom into which others may come by invitation only. At the foot of the stairs, bookshelves start at floor level and squishy cushions make an instant reading area.

At the other end of the apartment is a calm zone containing William and Trine's bedroom and bathroom; it is reached by a corridor separated from the central area by a door. 'With a family in a space this size, you definitely need somewhere quiet to retreat to,' says Trine. The corridor has been reconfigured as a dressing room; full-length cupboards papered in luxurious

hand-painted wallpaper conceal shelving and hanging space, and there is a mirror on the back of the door that connects with the reception area. Leading off the corridor is the simple and uncluttered master bedroom, and at the far end is a relaxing bathroom with French windows that open onto a luxurious decked terrace looking out over communal gardens.

When you have two young, very active children, it is not an easy task to design an apartment that works well on every level, but the Millers have shown that the careful planning of each space, no matter how small, can have triumphant results.

this page Beyond the bedroom is the main bathroom decorated in traditional manner with a wood-panelled bath, shower and a pair of basins set into a marble washstand, modelled on traditional French design. French windows, installed by the Millers, lead out onto a decked terrace overlooking communal gardens.

❏ **By using pale colour and soft patterns throughout, Trine Miller has miraculously managed to give this rambling apartment the feel of an English country house.**

❏ **Most of the loose covers, both in the sitting room and kitchen, are machine-washable – the only way to mix children and gracious living.**

❏ **Converting a corridor into a storage space for clothes, complete with hand-painted wallpaper, shows what can be done with unpromising areas.**

EASY ELEGANCE

In different hands, this New York apartment, in a 1930s building on Central Park, might have been merely a relic of a more gracious age; but its current owners have made it into a modern living space that is the height of elegance.

When the present owners moved in, they found that, as in many apartment buildings of the period, the rooms, particularly the reception rooms, were small and quite narrow, with lobbies and corridors connecting the spaces. The interior was also quite dark and the ceilings were low. The style of architecture and the arrangement of rooms were designed for a different age and a different way of life, but, rather than a major overhaul, what was required was the opening up of the whole area.

Unlike many New Yorkers, the owners did not want to live in a white box, so they decided to use colour to make the most of natural light and to enhance the sense of calm. They gave priority to a better arrangement of space, along with creating an illusion of width where little existed. It wasn't possible in a building of this period simply to knock everything down; lateral thinking and imaginative solutions were needed.

above left In a corner of the formal drawing room, metal, silver and Perspex are all used to help to reflect the light, which was in short supply.

left At the far end of the living room is a handsome glass-topped dining table with silver-leaf-rubbed wooden chairs.

right To give a visual impression of width, the sofa extends beyond the window to the far wall, where a single, decorative angel catches the eye.

For example, immediately facing, and quite close to, the front door was a structural wall that obviously could not come down. The design solution to this seemingly small but intractable problem was to install a large mirror on the wall, which opened up the space, enlarging it and giving it depth. Indeed, mirrors and glass are used all over the apartment to reflect light where it is needed. There were several doors in and around the lobby, which physically and visually cut down the space; they were all removed, and at once the space seemed lighter and larger.

When the owners first saw the apartment, what is now the main living room was two rooms: a conventional drawing room on the park side and a dining room at the end nearest the service quarters, separated from the lobby by a wall and doors. Like many other modern apartment-dwellers, they decided they would rather have one flowing space, so the wall was taken down and the room was redesigned – but visually rather than structurally. Now, instead of doors and walls, there is a vertical line running centrally

this page In what is a rather narrow room, visual tricks have been used to make the space appear wider. These include a wooden floor, unbroken by carpets or rugs, and a sofa that runs the length of the window wall with, behind it, curtains hung beyond the dimensions of the window.

opposite Off the hall that leads both to the drawing room and bedroom is a study that doubles as a small sitting room. Instead of a conventional door, it has sliding wooden screen doors – known as pocket doors – that disappear into the reveal when open. When the doors are closed, the frosted glass panels allow light through into the windowless hall area.

left The study's rich red colour palette both emphasizes its comfortable proportions and acts as a contrast to the silvery tones of the drawing room beyond.

below Subtle but sumptious luxury is the tone here. Beneath the coffered ceiling, the Knole sofa is covered in a rich Fortuny fabric; the curtains are soft, red and sheer; and the rug is made of thick, stitched felt.

down the length of the room, from the pier between the two windows to the far end of the room, with no rug to break the line. On the ceiling, in a modern interpretation of classical design, two circular mouldings have been added, one above the living area at the far end, the other echoing the circular dining table. The room is painted in soft silvery tones, with textured fabrics creating a subtle palette. Another linking device, and a clever take on the perennial storage issue, is a stretch of low, hidden cupboards running the length of the room, topped by a display shelf at mantel height; the shelf is made of marble and makes a fitting background for art and objects.

The room is not particularly wide and the window is off-centre; the owners resolved this visually by hanging curtains the length of the window wall – soft sheer drapes that gently diffuse the light, with blackout shades hidden underneath.

- **It is good to use colour in apartments, but it must be used subtly; loud clashes and harsh pairings rarely work.**

- **Mirrored furniture plays an important role in reflecting light at a lower level – a trick that can illuminate a room.**

- **In a narrow room with windows less than the width of the wall, make the room look larger by extending the curtains beyond the window edges.**

right Good-looking pieces of mirrored furniture, such as this mirrored chest of drawers, add to the reflective, aqueous feel of the room, while introducing a bit of old-fashioned Hollywood glamour.

Colour has been an important element in the reclaiming of this apartment. It has been applied lightly, tone on tone, rather than in a heavy-handed way, and is used consistently to complement any textiles that there may be in a room.

Next to the central living area, for example, is a warm, comfortable study and sitting room that has been painted in tones of deep, rich red. A small room, it was painted in this fashion to make it look larger and to draw attention to its inherent cosiness, emphasized by the rich Fortuny fabric on the Knole sofa. The imposing doorway appears intricately moulded but it lacks the traditional door that might be expected. Instead, a deep reveal within the moulding hides a pair of heavy sliding doors, designed with frosted glass panels in wood surrounds. The combination of the Oriental-style red paint and the wood-framed panels gives it an almost Japanese look. In practical terms, the design means that, even when the glass panels are closed to give privacy to the room's occupants, some light still penetrates the rest of the space.

The apartment's master bedroom and its connecting bathroom are also a symphony of subtle colour. In complete contrast to the small sitting room, the tones are light and silvery, pale and aqueous, made more so by the subtle turquoise moiré sheer curtains, hung over a paler plain fabric – a combination that gives a softer appearance than a single fabric used on its own. In the bathroom, mirrors, marble and tiny mosaic tiles, some of which are iridescent, contribute to the overall sense of watery peace.

There are so many different ideas, so many subtle touches, to be seen in this warm apartment, but all are presented in such a way as to act as a background to the owners' personalities and lives, rather than the other way around.

LAVISH L-SHAPE

David Collins excels at the sweeping design statement; justly renowned for his restaurant interiors, he shows the same attention to detail when it comes to apartments.

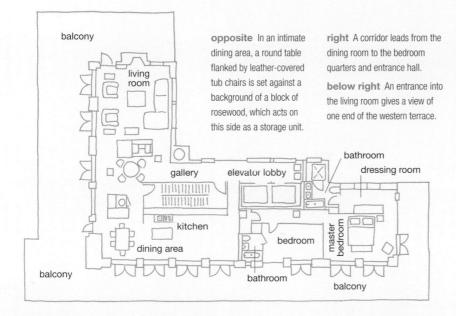

opposite In an intimate dining area, a round table flanked by leather-covered tub chairs is set against a background of a block of rosewood, which acts on this side as a storage unit.

right A corridor leads from the dining room to the bedroom quarters and entrance hall.

below right An entrance into the living room gives a view of one end of the western terrace.

balcony

living room

gallery

elevator lobby

bathroom

dressing room

kitchen

dining area

bedroom

master bedroom

bathroom

balcony

balcony

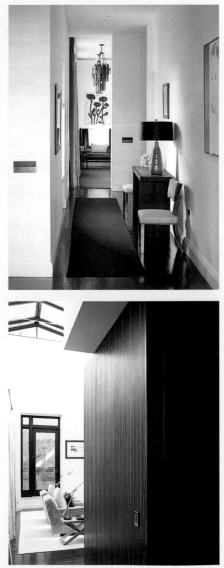

This penthouse apartment belongs to a businessman based in Los Angeles who divides his time between the East and West coasts. Until he found the apartment, he had always stayed in hotels when visiting New York, but this building represented an opportunity not to be missed. Designed in the distinctive style of the traditional apartment buildings and warehouses of Manhattan's Lower West Side, it had none of the problems that have to be taken into account when converting a former industrial space. It also had the advantage of being surrounded on all four sides by a broad terrace; one side of the apartment – with three sides of terrace – was a made-in-heaven entertaining space.

David Collins's brief was to design an integrated space that was simply decorated and easy to maintain – an archetypal pied-à-terre, albeit on a scale rarely encountered in the more modest interpretations of the phrase. It was also to be a place of refuge and privacy but, paradoxically, one that could also be used to entertain on a relatively lavish scale. This potentially contradictory combination of privacy and parties was an issue that

this picture This imposing living room is distinctive for its striking proportions. The chimney piece and mirror, both of which were specially designed for the room, act as a dramatic focus.

David had to address straightaway, and, although the building was purpose built, it was not an easy space to design. As David says, 'The layout is an elongated L-shape, which meant that there were long corridors and circulation spaces. I wanted to bring these spaces – or, if you like, areas that flow into one other – into the overall theme of the apartment and to make sure that guests who came to parties could feel free to roam around the apartment.' It was equally important that the bedroom side be closed off and private, which was achieved by designing almost concealed doors that break the apartment into two.

above Designed to be both classical and timeless, these custom-made chairs are upholstered in water-green velvet.

top The living-room side of the dividing unit is designed for storage and display. It holds audiovisual equipment as well as books and decorative objects.

Now, a long corridor leading through the centre of the apartment separates the hidden bedroom area from the public area. At the far end of the corridor is a circular dining table and chairs in an area that, according to David, acts as the formal dining room: 'It also doubles as a meeting space and somewhere where board meetings can take place if necessary.'

The enormous block of rosewood at one side of the table, which is actually a two-sided, multi-purpose storage and display unit, serves as a divider between the dining area and the entertaining area and reflects one of the design themes in the apartment. 'We worked on using the idea of blocks of rosewood and mahogany which form some of the cores of the media unit and the guest cloakrooms,' says David. 'These are being used as almost a sculptural divider – inspired a bit by the work of Donald Judd, although you might not think so at first!'

On the other side of the rosewood unit from the dining area is the showstopping space that dominates this end of the apartment: the living room – a poor description for such a striking room that incorporates tall French windows on each of the three sides. At its centre is a fireplace that was specially made for the apartment, as was the mirror above it. The colour palette – which appears in subtle variations throughout the apartment – includes greens, sapphire blues, gold and silver, colours that are used in a variety of fabrics ranging from velvets to woven silks and even silk carpets. The textiles are offset by a neutral palette of wall finishes, created by

left Made by Boffi, this ultra-modern reflective kitchen could as easily be used by professional cooks organizing a large celebration as by someone cooking a simple supper.

above At the far side of the kitchen table is a shelf unit that is as much for display as it is for storage – a feature that is in keeping with the chic feeling of the rest of the room.

- ❏ **Any apartment, large or small, needs a sense of 'flow'; it should be easy to get from one area to another without too many obstacles in between.**

- ❏ **Space that flows can be achieved both by design and, in some cases, by decorative aids.**

- ❏ **In a large apartment, simplicity of line is paramount – surprisingly, even more so than in a small space.**

mixing plaster and travertine dust, which creates an effect that is warm, sophisticated and luxurious. At first glance, the furniture in the apartment, such as the well-designed armchairs in this big room, seems very simple. Only on further inspection do you realize that, although the style may be simple, the realization definitely is not. In David's words, 'A lot of six-ply silk and cashmere was used.' The idea was to achieve a look that was classical, indulgent and super-comfortable but not too reminiscent of a 'bachelor pad'. It was important that the design of the furniture had a timeless quality and that the pieces looked as if they had been there for some time, rather than suffering from 'developer's finish' – a fate not unknown in other newly decorated New York apartments.

On the other side of the dining area, a state-of-the-art kitchen has been installed featuring white lacquer and marble worktops, and made by Boffi. 'Again, it was very much inspired by the idea of a kitchen which looks good enough to eat in but also has a very "luxe" feel,' explains David. 'Lacquer and marble are designed more often for the use of external caterers preparing food for a fabulous party rather than for ordinary people actually doing some hard-graft cooking. I wanted the kitchen space to be quite chic and designed, but not too cold and minimal.'

At the heart of the apartment is the media unit – the client's personal working zone – which also features large blocks of wood, this time mahogany, designed as storage and working spaces. Beyond that, at the other end of the apartment, is the almost totally private bedroom zone. Apart from a small, pretty bedroom for the client's daughter, there is, in the far corner, the master bedroom with windows and terraces on two sides. This is a haven of silky calm, from which a dressing corridor – as opposed to a dressing room – leads down to the sort of bathroom that you would never want to leave. The colours are subdued and peaceful, the textures soft and luxurious.

'The bedrooms may appear simple,' says David, 'but there are luxurious touches to be seen in the detail of the fabrics – the use of cashmere and printed silks, especially embossed leathers, and some custom-designed furniture that give a bespoke quality feeling. I find that many apartments in New York, especially those located downtown in SoHo or TriBeCa, have a strongly "industrial" feel. I wanted to soften this Americanization with the more European feel of luxury and classicism.' This apartment is a work in progress, a place that, according to David, will evolve as time goes on. It is, as he says, a timeless design, and one that can only get better.

above This classically designed bathroom encompasses a shower that could well be a room on its own, complete with Roman-style bench and an alcove cut into the wall for storing bottles and pots.

above left A corner of the bathroom reveals the large bath with centrally placed taps and the generous double basin unit with hinged mirrors at either end.

opposite, left In the bedroom, the wall behind the bed stops short of the outside wall, making the entrance to a dressing corridor that leads to the bathroom and is lined with clothes cupboards and shelves.

opposite, right The bedroom, which has its own terrace beyond, is simply, even sparsely, furnished, with an easy chair and a single rosewood dressing chest.

DISPLAY SPACE

this page To the right of the entrance foyer is the sitting zone of this large loft space. Club chairs by Milo Baughman and the unusual rug, with a design of tonally different circles, ties the area together. The set of photographs behind the sofa are by Vic Muniz.

Yancey and Mark Richardson have lived in this apartment for three years, but their plans for it date back much further, since not only did they rent the neighbouring apartment but, for a while, Mark used what is now their home as a work space.

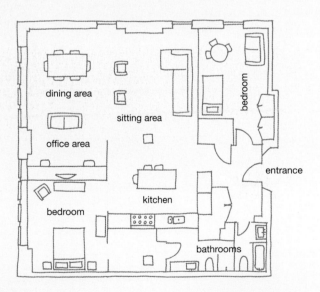

dining area

sitting area

office area

bedroom

kitchen

bedroom

entrance

bathrooms

When this former industrial space was turned into a condominium, the Richardsons were able to buy it. Yancey is an art dealer and gallery owner with a particular interest in 20th-century photography, so it made perfect sense for her to ask Michael Stevens of Stevens Learner, a firm of architects who specialize in the design and renovation of gallery space, to oversee the apartment project. Not that the Richardsons wanted to live in a gallery, of course, but they did want to be able to display some of their large collection, as well as to change things around from time to time. While agreeing that he could fulfil their wishes, Michael pointed out that it would not be possible to light every piece of art as if it were in a gallery, but that they could still create walls that they could re-hang when they wanted to. So the space had to be flexible; it also had to be home for Yancey and Mark and their nine-year-old daughter.

As Yancey says, 'The space has to deliver enough room for everyone to be comfortable. We wanted it to have a fluid, clean-lined look, contemporary but warm and homely – which actually is what so many people want.'

Michael Stevens was pleased to take on the project: 'I like working with art people because we speak the same language, and it makes sense if you employ an architect or designer to know that they are on your wavelength.'

this picture An overview of the living space shows the kitchen zone to the left, with a painting by Vic Muniz on the wall, and the bedroom beyond. On the far side of the seating area is the partially divided study and television zone, showing the integrated desk and television unit installed against the wall.

this page Two square leather stools sit in front of the unit that incorporates an office and book shelves. On the wall is a work by Adam Fuss. The three nudes on the desk are by Alvin Booth.

With hindsight, there seems to have been a natural sequence of events in the way that the design of the apartment evolved, but – although it might appear easier when planning an apartment to have just a single large space to play with – it can be more challenging if there are no existing parameters to work within.

In this case, as so often happens in converted industrial spaces, the position of the services informed the layout of the rest of the apartment. As Yancey says, 'The planning of the interior was actually pretty clear. It would have been very difficult to move the plumbing, so that meant that the kitchen area had to be where it is now, which in turn meant that there would be a bathroom on the other side of the kitchen, which in turn meant that the master bedroom would have to lead off that, as well as leading back into the main space.'

With those basic questions answered, the rest of the discussion centred on the best use of the rest of the space. Did they want the dining area close to the kitchen? And where would they put a work space for Mark that would give him enough privacy and yet not be completely cut off from the rest of the living area?

'I was keen to have the dining area a little further away from the kitchen so that no traces of cooking or dishes could be seen when you were at the table,' says Yancey. 'We were concerned about whether putting it the other side of the

above The dining zone at the far end of the living space is designed in a way that allows it to stand alone within the context of the whole area. On the wall is a set of nine pool pictures by Ed Ruscha that define the area.

space would work well, but it does.' With the seating area closer to the kitchen and the entrance to the apartment, there is now a sense of movement as guests walk from the sofas across to the table. Then there was Mark's space to think about, where the television was also meant to be located. 'That was a big challenge, as we tried to work out how to squeeze in the television, the books, the music and a desk. At first we looked at putting the study where the sitting area is, but it didn't work, so we decided to do it as a built-in area on the other side of the room. At one point,

above and left The bedroom leads directly off the kitchen, which is a better arrangement than it sounds. Simply furnished, the bedroom has a dresser by Russell Wright and four panel colour photographs by David Hilliard.

right A wall of tiles with a soft, almost translucent, blue glaze, the frosted shelf doors and the old painted dresser combine to give the kitchen a watery feel.

below A sliding door separates the kitchen from the bedroom — all that is needed in this area of integrated spaces and zones.

this page In the bedroom, the beside chest echoes the larger version of the dressing corridor that leads to the bathroom. Behind the bed is a colour landscape by Elger Esser, and on the far wall is a nude by Sally Mann.

there was an enclosing wall on the plan, until I realized that the wall would cut off light from the rest of the apartment. The study was intended to be private but to block it off entirely would have been too drastic. Where to put the television was a big decision. Should it be the bedroom, the living room, the study? Luckily, television sets are becoming more discreet, and we managed to integrate it into the shelving unit in the study.'

It is usual in this kind of industrial space to have at least one structural pillar; some try to hide it, some to integrate it. Yancey and Mark decided to make it into an architectural punctuation – something that defined the area, breaking up the space between kitchen and sitting zone.

Yancey also felt strongly about the entrance. 'I wanted a foyer. In my old apartment I had one, and I feel that it is good to walk into a transitional space – a place where packages can be left. A foyer brings a traditional element into what is essentially a loft space. It is also a contrast to everything else, so we deliberately painted it a darker colour than the other walls.'

Colour has been carefully considered throughout. Although white predominates, there is also a complementary palette of olive green, moleskin, terracotta and khaki, with the kitchen area in a palette of soft, almost watery tones. One-stop living is not conducive to clever colour contrasts, and the aim here was to create and define zones in an unobtrusive way.

The final element was the furniture, which Yancey wanted to choose herself: 'We were pretty involved in the design element of it all, and much of the furniture I found at a local gallery, Lobel Modern, which specializes in mid-20th-century pieces.' The art was chosen separately. 'It's buying the piece and then working out where to hang it.' The curtains, a double layer of moiré silk, were also designed and chosen by Yancey – 'I wanted something with a material lusciousness to it and a depth.'

It is clear that all this careful thought, together with the combined creative efforts of architect and client, has paid off. The apartment is comfortable and well planned, with objects of interest around every corner. A loft with brio, you might say!

above The narrow bathroom, which shares a partition wall with the kitchen, has a shower area at the far end that is separated from the rest of the room by a half-width glass screen. The basin's gooseneck tap is reflected in the mirror door.

❑ **It is impressive just how well the space has been thought through in this apartment. Every zone blends seamlessly into the next.**

❑ **In what was an industrial space, the Richardsons have made good use of the vast wall area to hang and display their art to best advantage.**

❑ **The furniture, including many key 20th-century designs, has been chosen as carefully as the art; the attention to detail brings its rewards.**

DISCREET CHARM

Some see luxury as elegant discretion, a hidden standard of perfection that leaves visible only the chic top notes. This Paris apartment exemplifies such subtle perfection.

Before restoration, this apartment looked very different from how it looks today. Situated on the top floor of a slightly dilapidated 19th-century apartment building on the left bank of the River Seine, it was old-fashioned to a fault and, although it had huge potential, including ravishing views of the Seine and the Musée d'Orsay, the interior had not been touched for 50 years. This was an apartment waiting to happen.

The client, a young European businessman, briefed interior designer Tino Zervudachi of Mlinaric, Henry & Zervudachi (MHZ) to create for him a stylish and original 'hotel suite' pied à terre in which he could relax and entertain. The other requirement was that the project had to be completed quickly – he wanted to move in as soon as possible.

Reached through a dark lobby, the main living area consisted of two rooms with a corridor; to the other side of the lobby was a small, impractical, unconverted kitchen. The first challenge was how to deal with such a warren of disconnected, narrow rooms made even smaller by the long, narrow corridor that blocked out the light. Although, looking at

above The front door once led into a small lobby, off which was a corridor that ran down one side of the apartment. It now opens directly into one large room, converted from two smaller ones.

opposite Beyond the sitting area of the room is the study, which can also be used as a dining space when necessary. The console between the two sofas holds a projector that projects images onto a screen lowered from the beam between the sitting and study areas.

overleaf The view down the room away from the study shows, on the right, the location of the corridor linking the three rooms that were there previously. To the left of the fireplace is a mirrored door that leads to the bedroom.

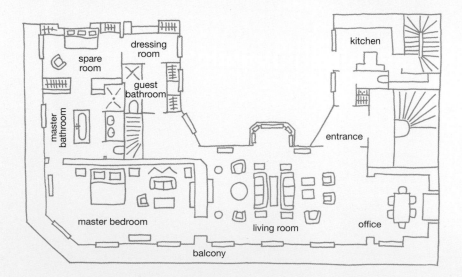

spare room

dressing room

guest bathroom

master bathroom

master bedroom

balcony

living room

kitchen

entrance

office

the result, the answer seems obvious, it was not so at the time. 'The problems were those of scale and symmetry,' says Antoine de Sigy, the MHZ designer who worked on the project with Tino. 'The conundrum was all about flow and the arrangement of space. With the client's input, we decided that the way to make the space work was to open it up – to take out the lobby, to remove the corridor walls and see what we were left with.'

Designer and client had also agreed that the apartment would benefit from the highest of high-tech electronics – not that these installations are at all obvious now. Air conditioning and heating would be hidden, the former behind the cornices, with the units and the controls in the recessed panels between the windows. There would be electronic controls for the lighting, the blackout blinds and the exterior retractable awnings. The tracks of the curtains (also electronically controlled) would be hidden in the cornice. In order to house the electronic controls, the recesses themselves had to be deepened – something that makes good aesthetic sense since it gives scale to the tall windows.

Part of the living area was designed for television and film viewing. In the beam that divides the sitting area from the working/dining alcove, there is a hidden screen that

above Comfortable chairs flank the re-centred fireplace designed by Tino Zervudachi. The opening-up of the space brings light and a perspective to the whole area.

below right Instead of the corridor that used to be here, the way through to the far staircase is delineated by a pair of console tables either side of an alcove furnished with a comfortable, deep window seat.

opposite Red leather chairs are grouped around a magical table of lights, designed by Ingo Maurer, with a pendant light above, also by Ingo Maurer.

❏ **What Tino did so cleverly in this large but badly planned space was to simplify ruthlessly: something from which many an apartment, large or small, would benefit.**

❏ **Removing an entire corridor altered not only the layout but also the light and the proportions of the rooms.**

❏ **The controls for everything, from the air conditioning to the exterior awnings and even the drop-down projector, are cunningly concealed.**

this picture At the entrance to the bedroom is a small but luxurious sitting area with a working fireplace. The pictures above the fireplace are by Julian Opie.

drops at the touch of a button. Between the two back-to-back sofas is a custom-made unit that holds a projector; at a touch of another button, it rises from the unit – and the armchairs swivel smoothly around for relaxed, easy viewing.

Instead of a traditional dining table, MHZ installed a table by Ingo Maurer, with soft pinpoints of light within its glassy depths, that can be used for both working and eating.

The kitchen now is super-smart. Small, functional and white apart from a dark brown countertop and dark brown blinds, it is a triumph of function: the kitchen that doesn't want to be noticed.

The master bedroom, off the living room, was originally two rooms. Today it looks perfectly proportioned, with windows that face both east and south, and a small sitting area in front of the fireplace. It opens onto the bathroom, which must be one of the most glamorous in Paris: all reflections from marble and mirrors

above The bedroom, once two rooms, was realigned and made into one well-proportioned room. There are windows running the length of the room as well as a curved one on the corner that looks south-east.

this page Leading off the bedroom is a bathroom with, in the best of luxurious traditions, a centrally placed bath set on a polished white marble floor. The bath has been placed in this position to suit the plumbing, but is none the less dramatic for that.

with a freestanding bath surrounded by marble and set in the centre of the room. It was a difficult room to design, says Antoine, since there was very little room for manoeuvre; nothing was centred and none of the services could be moved, as this was originally another bathroom. Leading off the bathroom is a dressing room with a sofa bed and deep, luxurious cupboards and wardrobes.

To the right of the fireplace in the main living area is a small hall, from which a staircase with a balustrade designed by Tino Zervudachi leads up to a guest suite above. This was originally three small attic rooms – the traditional *chambres de bonnes*, found in many traditional Parisian apartment buildings. It was decided to incorporate them into the main apartment, and the space now consists of a compact

bedroom, designed like a stateroom on a cruiser, and a remarkable grotto-like bathroom designed to make the most of the angles of the eaves, covered as it is from ceiling to floor in tiny mosaic tiles from Bisazza. The design had to be done in situ so that each area could be worked out and then gauged for effectiveness.

What is particularly interesting about this apartment is that so much thought and design work has gone into the space, but you really can't see it. But perhaps that is the definition of good design.

above left Along the wall is a wide, glassed shower enclosure, next to the recessed basin enclosure, which has a glamorous range of mirrored drawers that reflect the light from the tall windows.

right Compact and functional, the kitchen, to the right of the entrance, is designed with a white floor, white walls and dark surfaces – the perfect apartment kitchen.

above The dressing room that leads off the bathroom has a comfortable sofa that also doubles as a bed.

above left A chair in the sunny windows of the bathroom, beside the entrance to the dressing room, adds a luxurious touch. The door to the dressing room is designed to line up with the door into the bedroom.

SHEER ARTISTRY

Vicente Wolf is renowned for his disciplined, well-planned interior design, but the transformation he has achieved in this particular Manhattan apartment is truly staggering.

When Scott and Jodie Markoff moved in two years ago, the apartment, surprisingly for a covetable Central Park West address, had not been touched for more than 40 years. It is not a small apartment, although it was hard to see just how large it really was, as the whole area was split up into a series of small rooms, some of which were bedrooms, others a series of reception rooms and a kitchen. As the space stretches from the central well of the building to the street front, the only source of natural light was from the windows on the street side. This meant that most of the rooms were dark, and the reconfiguration of the space was an urgent priority. Jodie and Scott have two school-age boys so their wish was to have an apartment that would suit the needs of every member of the family – not an easy brief.

The first job was internal demolition. Once the partition walls of the small rooms had been taken down, Vicente was left with two fairly distinct spaces. The first, larger, space would hold the cooking, dining and living areas; while the second space, holding the bedrooms and bathrooms, would run parallel to the first, and would be reached from the other side of the hall, opposite the entrance door.

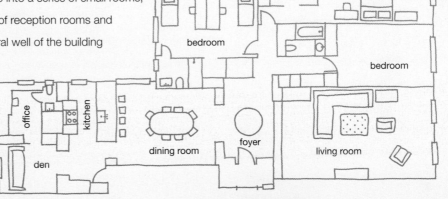

left From the dining table there is a view of the lighter sitting zone, across the lobby, delineated by a raised floor area.

this page At the far end of the living area – the only part to benefit from substantial daylight – is a group of chairs and a sofa. Beside the sofa, in an interesting juxtaposition, is an antique Burmese writing desk and a moulded 20th-century plastic chair.

above The wall on which the hob is installed has units built in varying degrees of depth – a design device to add interest to the kitchen end of the living area.

right From the dining table through to the working area, the clever eye-level display shelf can be seen running along the wall on the left.

left Looking away from the kitchen area, the quirky table, the eclectic collection of chairs and the open storage unit make for an easy transition to the rest of the living area.

❏ **Do think about the sources of daylight in an apartment and whether you can increase it by altering the layout of the space. Maximize what you have with lightweight curtains or blinds.**

❏ **If choosing a relatively neutral colour palette to make the most of the space, avoid a bland effect by adding some interesting furniture and unusual objects and pictures.**

The length of the main area – consisting of kitchen, dining room, hall and living room – meant that the floors were of major importance. Jodie Markoff was keen to have dark wenge wood, Vicente preferred pale Russian oak. The professional's view won and Jodie now recognizes its merits, since the oak reflects daylight in a way that a dark-toned wood would not. Since the new space stretched so far, it was important to avoid the impression of an undulating plain of wooden floor, and Vicente addressed this problem by staggering the floor levels so that the eye has an impression of varying scale.

He started with the area inside the entrance door, which opens into the centre of the apartment at a midway point. This was to be a hall-without-walls, that is to say a foyer, defined by an inset central panel of roughened slate, on which stands an antique drum table. He constructed a raised step, made of slate to match the inset panel, that leads down to, and now defines, the living area. This small feature totally alters the look of the apartment since the kitchen, at the opposite end, is on a slightly higher level than the living area, which makes it an important element in the overall design.

The eating and kitchen area, to the left of the foyer, was a crucial element to Jodie. Not only is she a good cook, but also, when two young boys are part of the household, food and everything to do with it is very important. An extra-long dining table – made from imported floorboards from the Philippines set on a modern base – acts as a transition to the working end of the room. Running the length of the wall at this end is a head-height, shallow-lipped ledge – a display area for Jodie's own work and for a changing display of other art as well as family photographs and decorative items.

The kitchen itself is of simple design but effective. It consists of a professional cooking range and ovens on the far wall with, facing out into the rest of the room, an island unit with a zinc top and, slightly incongruously, bulbous mahogany legs. Set into the unit is a large preparation area and sinks. The wall-hung units at the back of the kitchen are not of uniform depth, some extending further into the room than others, a feature that adds interest to what otherwise would have been a bland wall of cupboards and shelves.

At the other end of the apartment, the comfortable, spacious living area is defined by a subtle, sheer curtain which is hung between an antique cupboard and the sofa that faces the window. The space is furnished in soothing neutral tones and textures. Vicente and Jody looked for

right In the master bedrrom, the imposing bed head is a dark-stained fretwork screen backed by mirror – a striking idea, and one that is comparatively easy to copy.
far right The sleek bathroom, although narrow, is very well designed and consists of a mirrored basin area that leads to a glassed, roomy shower enclosure.

durable surfaces with furnishing fabrics that, although elegant, would be hard-wearing; the sofa, for example, is covered in a textured taupe mohair that conceals scuffs and marks. There is a combination of pieces chosen by Jody and others designed by Vicente, such as the comfortable tub armchair. The windows are hung with scrim fold-up blinds that diffuse the light.

The three bedrooms with dressing rooms and bathrooms were again formed out of the original clutter of small rooms. The master bedroom leads into a cool, well-lit bathroom with a dressing room carved out of a narrow sliver of space beside it that has been transformed into an area of precision storage.

Storage has been carefully considered throughout the apartment: from the shallow cupboard of shelves next to the entrance, which hold gloves and hats, scarves and other New York essentials, to the carefully designed, commodious dressing rooms. It is now a real New Yorker's apartment: elegant, well dressed and incredibly hard working.

PICTURE CREDITS

Key: **ph**=photographer; **a**=above, **b**=below, **r**=right, **l**=left, **c**=centre. Photography by Winfried Heinze except where stated otherwise.

Endpapers Florence & John Pearse's apartment in London; **1** Jodi and Scott Markoff's home, designer Vicente Wolf; **2** The apartment of Lars Kristensen, owner of Fil de Fer, Copenhagen; **3** Jodi and Scott Markoff's home, designer Vicente Wolf; **4** Florence & John Pearse's apartment in London; **5l** Jodi and Scott Markoff's home, designer Vicente Wolf; **5c** The apartment of Lars Kristensen owner of Fil de Fer, Copenhagen; **5r** Private residence, New York, designed by David Collins Studio; **6** Florence & John Pearse's apartment in London; **7–8** A Parisian apartment designed by Tino Zervudachi and Antoine de Sigy; **10l** Interior stylist Sidsel Zachariassen; **10c&r** Private residence, New York, designed by David Collins Studio; **11** The apartment of Yancey and Mark Richardson in New York. Architecture and Interior Design by Steven Learner Studio (photographs: Ed Ruscha); **12l ph** Chris Everard/Adèle Lakdari's home in Milan; **12–13** Trine and William Miller's home in London; **14 ph** Chris Everard/Designed by Mullman Seidman Architects; **15l ph** Jan Baldwin/Alfredo Paredes & Brad Goldfarb's loft in Tribeca, New York designed by Michael Neumann Architecture; **15ar ph** Jan Baldwin/The Fitzwilliam-Lay's family home. Architecture by Totem Design, interior design by Henry Fitzwilliam-Lay and Totem Design; **15br ph** Chris Everard/An apartment in New York designed by Mullman Seidman Architects; **16al ph** Christopher Drake/Karen Fisher of Designer Previews home in New York; **16bl** Christopher Drake/Suze Orman's apartment in New York designed by Patricia & Monika Brugger of Mullman Seidman Architects; **16r ph** Jan Baldwin/The Campbell family's apartment in London, architecture by Voon Wong Architects; **17 ph** Chris Everard/An actor's London Home designed by Site Specific; **18l** Claire Richardson/Fabric by Sanderson; **18r ph** Christopher Drake/Suze Orman's apartment in New York designed by Patricia & Monika Brugger of Mullman Seidman Architects; **19 ph** Andrew Wood/Mikko Puotila's apartment in Espoo, Finland. Interior design by Ulla Koskinen; **20** Trine and William Miller's home in London; **21a** The apartment of Lars Kristensen owner of Fil de Fer, Copenhagen; **21bl ph** Debi Treloar/Nicky Phillips' apartment in London; **21bc ph** Jan Baldwin/The Campbell family's apartment in London, architecture by Voon Wong Architects; **21br ph** Jan Baldwin/The owner of Tessuti, Catherine Vindevogel-Debal's house in Kotrijk, Belguim. Kitchen designed by Filip Van Bever; **22al ph** Chris Everard/Designed by Mullman Seidman Architects; **22ac ph** Chris Everard/Jo Warman – Interior Concepts; **22ar ph** Claire Richardson/Barbara Zorn of Atelier LZC's flat in Paris/Cushions, prints on wall and furniture, ceramics and glassware by Atelier LZC; **22b** Private residence, New York, designed by David Collins Studio; **24al ph** Chris Everard/Jo Warman – Interior Concepts; **24bl ph** Andrew Wood/Andrew Duncanson's (owner of Modernity) apartment in Stockholm, Sweden; **24r ph** Chris Everard/Jo Warman – Interior Concepts; **25l** The Notting Hill flat of Ebba Thott from 'Sigmar' in London; **25ar ph** Chris Everard/Jo Warman – Interior Concepts; **25br** Florence & John Pearse's apartment in London; **26a ph** Chris Everard/Suze Orman's apartment in New York designed by Patricia & Monika Brugger of Mullman Seidman Architects; **26bl ph** Debi Treloar/Belén Moneo & Jeff Brock's apartment in New York by Moneo Brock Studio; **26br ph** Chris Everard/Mullman Seidman Architects; **27** Trine and William Miller's home in London; **28a** The home of Christian Permin and Kamilla Byriel of Stella Nova, in Copenhagen; **28b ph** Jan Baldwin/A family home in Parsons Green, London. Architecture by Nicholas Helm and Yasuyuki Fukuda (architectural assistant) of Helm Architects. Interior design and all material finishes supplied by Maria Speake of Retrouvius Reclamation & Design; **29** A Parisian pied-à-terre designed by Marianne Pascal for an Anglo-French couple; **30–31 ph** Polly Wreford/Peri Wolfman and Charles Gold's New York Loft; **31r ph** Jan Baldwin/Peter & Nicole Dawes' apartment, designed by Mullman Seidman Architects; **32** Jodi and Scott Markoff's home, designer Vicente Wolf; **33al ph** Jan Baldwin/Alfredo Paredes & Brad Goldfarb's loft in Tribeca, New York, designed by Michael Neumann Architecture; **33bl ph** Christopher Drake/Antique dealer and co-owner of Jamb Ltd/antique chimney pieces; **33r ph** Jan Baldwin/Architect Joseph Dirand's apartment in Paris; **34a ph** Chris Everard/An actor's London home designed by Site Specific; **34b ph** Christopher Drake/Antique dealer and co-owner of Jamb Ltd/antique chimney pieces; **35 ph** Chris Everard/Central Park West Residence, NYC designed by Bruce Bierman Design, Inc; **36** A Parisian apartment designed by Tino Zervudachi and Antoine de Sigy; **37a ph** Chris Everard/Christopher Coleman's New York apartment; **37b ph** Jan Baldwin/Interior designer Didier Gomez's apartment in Paris; **38l ph** Christopher Drake/Antique dealer and co-owner of Jamb Ltd/antique chimney pieces; **38r ph** Chris Everard/An apartment in Paris designed by Bruno Tanquerel; **39** The home of Hernando and Gigi Pérez in New York City; **40** A Parisian apartment designed by Tino Zervudachi and Antoine de Sigy; **41al ph** Chris Everard/Monique Witt & Steven Rosenblum, Mullman Seidman Architects; **41cl ph** Jan Baldwin/Christopher Leach's apartment in London; **41ar ph** Andrew Wood/Mikko Puotila's apartment in Espoo, Finland. Interior design by Ulla Koskinen; **41b ph** Chris Everard/designed by Mullman Seidman Architects; **42l ph** Chris Everard/Interior designer Alan Tanksley's own apartment in Manhattan; **42ar ph** Chris Everard/Richard Hopkin's apartment in London designed by HMZ; **42br ph** Jan Baldwin/Christopher Leach's apartment in London; **43** Jodi and Scott Markoff's home, designer Vicente Wolf; **44l** The apartment of Lars Kristensen owner of Fil de Fer, Copenhagen; **44c** The apartment of Jacques Azagury in London; **44r** The home of Hernando and Gigi Pérez in New York City; **45** A Parisian pied-à-terre designed by Marianne Pascal for an Anglo-French couple; **46** The Notting Hill flat of Ebba Thott from 'Sigmar' in London; **47l** The apartment of Jacques Azagury in London; **47c** The apartment of Lars Kristensen owner of Fil de Fer, Copenhagen; **47r** The apartment of Jacques Azagury in London; **48–55** Interior stylist Sidsel Zachariassen; **56–61** The Notting Hill flat of Ebba Thott from 'Sigmar' in London; **62–69** A Parisian pied-à-terre designed by Marianne Pascal for an Anglo-French couple; **70–75** The apartment of Jacques Azagury in London; **76–85** The apartment of Lars Kristensen owner of Fil de Fer, Copenhagen; **86** Florence & John Pearse's apartment in London; **87l** The home of Christian Permin and Kamilla Byriel of Stella Nova, in Copenhagen; **87c & r** Florence & John Pearse's apartment in London; **94–101** Florence & John Pearse's apartment in London; **102–109** Signe Bindslev Henriksen of Space Architecture and Design; **110–19** The home of Christian Permin and Kamilla Byriel of Stella Nova, in Copenhagen of Stella Nova; **120** The apartment of Yancey and Mark Richardson in New York. Architecture and Interior Design by Steven Learner Studio; **121l** Private residence, New York, designed by David Collins Studio; **121c** The apartment of Yancey and Mark Richardson in New York. Architecture and Interior Design by Steven Learner Studio; **121r** Jodi and Scott Markoff's home, designer Vicente Wolf **122–31** Trine and William Miller's home in London; **132–37** The home of Hernando and Gigi Pérez in New York City; **138–45** Private residence, New York, designed by David Collins Studio; **146–55** The apartment of Yancey and Mark Richardson in New York. Architecture and Interior Design by Steven Learner Studio; **156–65** A Parisian apartment designed by Tino Zervudachi and Antoine de Sigy; **166–71** Jodi and Scott Markoff's home, designer Vicente Wolf; **176** Trine and William Miller's home in London.

BUSINESS CREDITS

Alan Tanksley
114 East 32nd St, Suite 1406
New York, NY 10016, USA
+ 1 212 481 8454
Page 42l.

Atelier LZC
2 rue Marcellin Berthelot
93100 Montreuil, France
+ 33 1 42 87 88 34
www.aterlierlzc.fr
Page 22ar.

Bruce Bierman Design
29 West 15th Street
New York, NY 10011, USA
+ 1 212 243 1935
www.biermandesign.com
Page 35.

Bruno Tanquerel, Artist
2 Passage St Sebastien
75011 Paris, France
+ 33 1 43 57 03 93
Page 38r.

**Christopher Coleman
Interior Design**
55 Washington Street
Suite 707
Brooklyn, NY 11021, USA
+ 1 718 222 8984
www.ccinteriordesign.com
Page 37a.

Christopher Leach Design
The Studio, 13 Crescent Place
London SW3 2EA
020 7235 2648
mail@christopherleach.com
Pages 40cl, 42br.

David Collins Studio
www.davidcollins.com
*Pages 5r, 10c & r, 22b,
121l, 138–45.*

Designer Previews
+ 1 212 777 2966
Page 16al.

Fil de Fer
St Kongensgade 83 A
1264 Copenhagen K
Denmark
+ 45 33 32 32 46
www.fildefer.dk
*Pages 2, 5c, 21a, 44l,
47c, 76–85.*

**Filip van Bever
Kitchen Design**
filipvanbever@skynet.be
Page 21br.

Helm Architects
2 Montagu Row
London W1U 6DX.
020 7224 1884
nh@helmarchitects.com
Page 28b.
and
**Retrouvius Reclamation
& Design**
2A Ravensworth Road
Kensal Green
London NW10 5NR
020 8960 6060
mail@helmarchitects.com
Page 28b.

Henri Fitzwilliam-Lay
Interior Design
hfitz@hotmail.com
Page 15ar.

HM2
33–37 Charterhouse Square
London EC1M 6EA
020 7600 5151
Andrew.hanson@
harper.mackay.co.uk
Page 42ar.

Interior Concepts
6 Warren Hall
Manor Road
Loughton
Essex IG10 4RP
020 8508 9952
www.jointeriorconcepts.co.uk
Pages 22ac, 24a, 25ar.

Jacques Azagury
50 Knightsbridge
London SW1X 7JN
020 7245 1216
www.jacquesazagury.com
Pages 44c, 47l&r, 70–75.

Jamb
Antique Chimneypieces
Core One
The Gas Works
Gate D, Michael Road
London SW6 2AN.
020 7736 3006
sales@jamblimited.com
Pages 33bl, 34b, 38l.

**Jeff Brock and
Belén Moneo**
Moneo Brock Studio
371 Broadway, 2nd Floor
New York, NY 10013, USA
+ 1 212 625 0308
Page 26bl.

John Pearse
6 Meard Street
London W1F OEG
020 7434 0738
www.johnpearse.co.uk
*Pages 4, 6, 25br, 86, 87c&r,
94–101 and endpapers.*

Joseph Dirand Architecture
338 rue des Pyrenees
75020 Paris, France
+ 33 1 47 97 78 57
joseph.dirand@wanadoo.fr
Page 33r.

**Laurent Bourgois
Architecte**
6 rue Basfroi
75011 Paris, France
Pages 7–8, 36, 40, 156–65.

Marianne Pascal Architecte
85 rue Albert
75013 Paris, France.
+ 33 1 45 86 60 01
www.mariannepascal.com
*Pages 24, 29, 45, 62–69,
88–93.*

**Michael Neumann
Architecture**
11 East 88th Street
New York, NY 10128, USA
+ 1 212 828 0407
www.mnarch.com
Page 15bl, 33ar.

**Mlinaric, Henry &
Zervudachi (MHZ)**
London: 020 7730 9072
Paris: + 33 1 42 96 08 62
www.mlinaric-henry-
zervudachi.com
Page 7–8, 36, 40, 156–65.

Modernity
Kopmangatan 3
111 31 Stockholm, Sweden
+ 46 8 20 80 25
www.modernity.se
Page 24bl.

**Mullman Seidman
Architects**
443 Greenwich Street
New York, NY 10013, USA
+ 1 212 431 0770
www.mullmanseidman.com
*Page 14, 15br, 16bl, 18r,
22ar, 26a & br, 31r, 41b.*

**Ory & Didier Gomez
Interior Design**
15 rue Henri Heine
75016 Paris, France
+ 33 1 44 30 88 23
orygomez@free.fr
Page 37b.

Peri Wolfman
Wolfman Gold
peri@charlesgold.com
Page 30–31.

Sidsel Zachariassen
Stenderupgade 1 1tv
1738 Copenhagen V
Denmark
www.sidselz.dk
Page 10l, 48–55.

Sigmar
263 Kings Road
London SW3 5EL
020 7751 5802
www.sigmarlondon.com
Pages 25l, 46, 55–61.

Site Specific
60 Peartree Street
London EC1V 3SB
020 7490 3176
www.sitesoecificltd.co.uk
Page 17, 34ar.

**Space Architecture
and Design**
sh@spacecph.dk
mail@spacecph.dk
+ 45 35 24 84 84/85
www.spacecph.dk
Page 102–109.

Steven Learner Studio
307 7th Avenue, Room 2201
New York, NY 10001, USA
+ 1 212 741 8583
www.stevenlearner
studio.com/index.htm>
*Pages 11, 120, 121c,
146–55.*

Stella Nova
Hauser Plads 32, 1st Floor
DK-1128 Copenhagen K
Denmark
+ 45 33 30 89 89
www.stella-nova.dk
Page 28a, 87l, 110–19.

Tessuti
Interiors & Fabrics
Doorniksewijk 76,
8500 Kortrijk, Belguim
+ 32 56 25 29 27
www.tessuti.be
Page 21br.

Totem Design
Ian Hume
2 Alexander Street
London W2 5NT
020 7243 0692
totem.uk@virgin.net
Page 15ar.

**Vicente Wolf
Associates**
333 West 39th Street
New York, NY 10018
USA
+ 1 212 465 0590
www.vicentewolf
associates.com
*Pages 1, 3, 5, 32, 43, 121r,
166–71.*

Voon Wong Architects
Unit 27
1 Stannary Street
London SE11 4AD
020 7587 0116
voon@btconnect.com
Page 16, 21bc.

Woodnotes OY
Tallberginkatu 1B
00180 Helsinki
Finland
+ 35 8 9694 2200
www.woodnotes.fi
Page 19, 41ar.

**Yancey Richardson
Gallery**
535 West 22nd Street
New York, NY 10011
USA
www.yancaeyrichardson.com
*Pages 11, 120, 121c,
146–55.*

INDEX

Note: All page numbers in *italics* refer to captions.

AUTHOR'S ACKNOWLEDGEMENTS

Apartment owners as a breed are generous with their time and hospitality, and eager to explain what exactly makes their homes so special. Many, many thanks to all those who let us in through their front doors and made us feel so welcome.

Thanks also to our photographer, Winfried Heinze – for his wonderful photographs, obviously, but also for immediately understanding the point of each apartment, never being fazed and always being cheerful. And many thanks to the seamless dream team at Ryland Peters & Small: Henrietta Heald, Jess Walton and Toni Kay, who made doing this book both problem-free and pleasurable.